THE LOGIC OF GOD

THE LOGIC OF GOD

52 CHRISTIAN ESSENTIALS FOR THE HEART AND MIND

RAVI ZACHARIAS

ZONDERVAN

The Logic of God: 52 Christian Essentials for the Heart and Mind

Copyright © 2019 by Ravi Zacharias

This title is also available as a Zondervan ebook.

This title is also available as a Zondervan audio book.

Requests for information should be addressed to:
Zondervan, 3900 Sparks Dr. SE, Grand Rapids, MI 49546.

ISBN 978-0-310-45403-8

Published in association with the literary agency of Wolgemuth & Associates, Inc.

Printed in the United States of America

19 20 21 22 23   LSC   10 9 8 7 6 5 4 3 2

*To my grandchildren, Jude, Ava, Isabella, Nico, and Jameson.
So young in their thinking and imagination now.
May their nurture in God's eternal truths make them blossom
into spiritual maturity to embrace the elegant,
wise, and perfect mind of God.*

CONTENTS

CONTENTS

CONTENTS

INTRODUCTION

Today, many people think it is naïve to believe in God because there is not enough evidence for His existence. Others conclude that even if He does exist, He has insufficiently revealed and inadequately explained Himself; therefore He has not convinced us that He is real. Even less has He affirmed that the claims of the gospel of Jesus Christ are true and lead to a worldview that offers the most coherent and logical answers to life's four essential questions—origin, meaning, morality, and destiny.

For the Christian this is where the battle must be fought, for no worldview suffers more from the loss of belief in God than the Christian one. And unless the "logic" of God—the evidence He has provided us of His existence—is defended, is sought after, is fully engaged with our hearts and minds, every essential of the Christian faith will be deemed illogical and untrue, thereby making them unworthy of rational assent.

The question then is, how does a person come to view this "logic" (this "evidence") as a reason to believe in a God on whom all other essentials of the Christian faith are built, by which life must be governed, and with which your personal beliefs, your culture, and the unique message of Jesus Christ are examined? The purpose of this book, and the way it is designed to be used, is to guide you on that journey. Here is a collection of my writings, most never before published in book form, selected for their perspective on the many ways God has provided us with evidence of His existence and how this "logic" gives life meaning, establishes the credibility of the Christian message, shows the weakness of modern intellectual movements, demonstrates the certainty of the claims of Jesus Christ, and validates biblical teaching and Christian apologetics.

Before you begin to engage with this material, let me give you a glimpse of the opportunity you have to experience this book in the most meaningful way. *The Logic of God* contains fifty-two readings. Each reading is preceded by a relevant quote from the Bible. I've added two other features to help you *reflect* on important themes in the readings (Reflection Questions) and *apply* the lessons learned from the readings (Personal Application).

Because these readings will consistently challenge your mind and stir your heart, and the questions and applications will take time to process, I recommend that, if possible, you spend a week with each "experience." If you start on a Monday, think of it as a kind of "Thank God It's Monday" summons, add that cliché to your intention, and thus help make your usual Mondays actually something to look forward to. Whatever motivates, right?

Okay. I know. A year is a big commitment. But the issues surrounding the subject of truth are serious business and have eternal consequences.

God wants us to know Him personally and live out our faith day by day in meaningful ways, but the noise, chaos, clutter, and busyness of life so often overwhelm that we find it difficult, if not impossible. We also can just routinely go through life not even conscious of His existence and end up trapped in a vicious cycle of wrong thinking and believing, and the cardinal statement of Jesus, "I am the way and the truth and the life," becomes meaningless.

Dear reader, thank you for beginning your personal journey with these fifty-two experiences, for in so doing you are demonstrating a desire to know God more deeply and walk in intimate oneness with Him through His Son, Jesus Christ. God wants you to be ever more confident that He is real, that He loves you and desires to fulfill all the longings of your heart.

With my prayers for your journey,

RAVI

BEHIND EVERY QUESTION

We implore you on Christ's behalf: Be
reconciled to God. God made him who had
no sin to be sin for us, so that in him we
might become the righteousness of God.

2 CORINTHIANS 5:20–21

We are living in an era when apologetics is indispensable, but at the same time, we need a Christian apologetic that is not merely heard—it must also be seen. The field of apologetics deals with the hard questions posed to the Christian faith. Having had deep questions myself, I listen carefully to the questions raised. I always bear in mind that behind every question is a questioner. The convergence of intellectual and existential struggles drives a person to a brutal honesty in the questions he or she has.

The gospel of Jesus Christ is beautiful and true, yet oftentimes one will ask, "How can it be true that there is only one way?" Odd, isn't it, that we don't ask the same questions of the laws of nature or of any assertion that lays claim to truth? We are discomfited by the fact that truth, by definition, is exclusive. That is what truth claims are at their core.

The question really is, *how do we know this is the truth?*

Whether religious or irreligious, everyone has a worldview. A worldview basically offers answers to four necessary questions: origin, meaning, morality, and destiny. In turn, these answers must be correspondingly true on particular questions and, as a whole, all answers put together must be coherent.

Taking it a step further, the three tests for truth must be applied to any worldview: logical consistency, empirical adequacy, and experiential relevance. When submitted to these tests, the Christian message is utterly unique and meets the demand for truth.

Consider the empirical test of the person, teaching, and work of Jesus Christ. A look at human history shows why He was who He claimed to be and why millions follow Him today. A comparison of Jesus' teachings with any other claimant to divine or prophetic status quickly shows the profound differences in their claims and demonstrations. In fact, none except Jesus even claimed to be the divine Savior. His offer of grace and forgiveness by being the perfect sacrifice of our offense—that "we might become the righteousness of God"—is profoundly unique.

I position the sequence of fact and deduction in the following way: (love is the supreme ethic. Where there is the possibility of love, there must be the reality of free will) Where there is the reality of free will, there will inevitably be the possibility of sin. Where there is sin, there is the need for a Savior. Where there is a Savior, there is the hope for redemption. Only in the Judeo-Christian worldview does this sequence find its total expression and answer. The story from sin to redemption is only in the gospel with the ultimate provision of a loving God.

The verification of what Jesus taught and described and did make belief in Him a very rationally tenable and an existentially fulfilling reality. From cosmology to history to human experience, the Christian faith presents explanatory power in a way no other worldview does. Our faith and trust in Christ are reasonably grounded and experientially sustained.

I was born to Indian parents and raised in India. My ancestors were priests from the highest caste of Hinduism in India's Deep South. But that was several generations ago. I came to Christ after a life of protracted failure and, unable to face the consequences, I sought to end it all. It was on a bed of suicide that a Bible was brought to me, and in a cry of desperation, I invited Jesus Christ into my life. It was a prayer, a plea, a commitment, and a hope.

I hardly knew what lay ahead of me, except that I was safe in Christ's hands. Now over fifty years later, I marvel at the grace of God and am convinced that Jesus Christ alone uniquely answers the deepest questions of our hearts and minds.

REFLECTION QUESTIONS

1. How does the idea that "behind every question is a questioner" affect your understanding of apologetics?
2. What does it mean to "become the righteousness of God," and how is the gospel unique among other worldviews?

PERSONAL APPLICATION

1. Is your faith in Jesus reasonably grounded and experientially sustained, or do you struggle with doubt? How might you address any doubts of the mind or heart this week?
2. When someone asks you to explain either why you go to church or why you are a Christian, how do you respond?

2

THE ULTIMATE CALLING

Be like-minded, be sympathetic, love one
another, be compassionate and humble.
Do not repay evil with evil or insult with
insult. On the contrary, repay evil with
blessing, because to this you were called
so that you may inherit a blessing. . . .
In your hearts revere Christ as Lord. Always
be prepared to give an answer to everyone
who asks you to give the reason for the hope
that you have. But do this with gentleness
and respect, keeping a clear conscience.

1 PETER 3:8–9, 15–16

A starting point for taking on the responsibility of the work of Christian apologetics is recognizing the role that living out a disciplined Christian life plays. Even a brief examination of the Scriptures reveals this striking imperative: one may not divorce the content of apologetics from the character of the apologist. *Apologetics* derives from the Greek word *apologia,* "to give an answer." First Peter 3:15 gives us the defining statement: "In your hearts revere Christ as Lord. Always be prepared to give an answer [*apologia*] to everyone who asks you to give the reason for the hope that you have. But do this with gentleness and respect."

I have always found this to be such a fascinating verse because the apostle Peter, under the inspiration of the Holy Spirit, knew the hazards and the risks of being an answer-bearer to the sincere questions people would pose of the gospel. Indeed, when one contrasts the answers of Jesus to those of any of His detractors, it is easy to see that their resistance is not of the mind but rather of the heart. Furthermore, I have little doubt that the single greatest obstacle to the impact of the gospel has not been its inability to provide answers, but the failure on our parts to live it out. The British evangelist Rodney "Gipsy" Smith once said, "There are five Gospels: Matthew, Mark, Luke, John, and the Christian, but most people will never read the first four."[1] In other words, apologetics is often first seen before it is heard.

For that very reason the Scriptures give us a clear picture of the apologetic Christian: one who has first set apart Christ in his or her heart as Lord, who responds with answers to the questioner with gentleness and respect. Therefore, one must not overlook the stark reality that the way one's life is lived out will determine the impact. Few obstacles to faith are as serious as expounding the unlived life. Too many simply see the quality of one's life and firmly believe that it is all theory, bearing no supernatural component.

I remember well in the early days of my Christian faith talking to a Hindu man. He was questioning the strident claims of the followers of Christ as being something supernatural. He absolutely insisted conversion was nothing more than a decision to lead a more ethical life, and that in most cases it was not any different to those claims of other "ethical" religions. So far, his argument was not anything new.

But then he said something I have never forgotten and often reflect upon: "If this conversion is truly supernatural, why is it not more evident in the lives of so many Christians I know?"

His question is a troublesome one. After all, no Buddhist claims a supernatural life but frequently lives a more consistent one. The same pertains to many of the other faiths. Yet, how often the so-called Christian, even while proclaiming some of the loftiest truths one could ever express, lives a life bereft of that beauty and character.

This call to a life reflecting the person of Christ is the ultimate calling upon the apologist. Skeptics are not slow to notice when there is a disparity, and because of that, may question the whole gospel in its supernatural claim. Yet when they are met with gentleness and respect, we will help meet the deepest longings of the heart and mind—and they will find where true discovery lies. Let us live so accordingly.

REFLECTION QUESTIONS

1. What does it look like to "revere Christ as Lord"? Why does Peter begin his charge with this injunction?
2. What is "the single greatest obstacle to the impact of the gospel," and what is so difficult about "expounding the unlived life"?

PERSONAL APPLICATION

1. How has your conversion experience made a visible difference in your life and in those around you?
2. What might you do this week to become a more effective witness for Christ?

3

POINT OF EXCLUSION

Thomas said to him, "Lord, we
don't know where you are going, so
how can we know the way?"
Jesus answered, "I am the way and the truth
and the life. No one comes to the Father
except through me."

With the numerous religions in the world, how can Christians claim exclusivity? I am often asked this question in different settings. But I've always been fascinated by the fact that the Christian faith is the only one that seems to have this question posed. The truth is that every religion has its starting points and its deductions, and those starting points exclude.

For example, Hinduism has two nonnegotiable beliefs: karma and reincarnation. No Hindu will trade these away. In Buddhism, there is the denial of the essential notion of the self. Buddhists believe that the self as we understand it does not exist, and our ceasing to desire will be the cause of the end of all suffering. If we deny these premises, we devein Buddhism.

Islam believes that Mohammad is the last and final prophet, and the Qur'an is the perfect revelation. If we deny those two premises, we have denied Islam. Even naturalism, which poses as irreligion, is exclusive. Naturalism teaches that anything supernatural or metaphysical is outside the realm of evidence and purely an opinion, not a matter of fact.

In the Christian faith, we believe Jesus is the consummate experience of God in the person of His Son and is the Savior and Redeemer of the world. We cannot deny these premises and continue to be Christians.

The question is not whether these are mutually exclusive. The question is, which one of these will we deny as being reasonable and consistent? Which one of these will we be able to sustain by argument and by evidence?

It is the very nature of truth that presents us with this reality. Truth by definition is exclusive. Everything cannot be true. If everything is true, then nothing is false. And if nothing is false, then it would also be true to say everything is false. We cannot have it both ways. One should not be surprised at the claims of exclusivity. The reality is that even those who deny truth's exclusivity, in effect, exclude those who do not deny it. The truth quickly emerges. The law of noncontradiction does apply to reality: two contradictory statements cannot both be true in the same sense. Thus, to deny the law of noncontradiction is to affirm it at the same time. You may as well talk about a one-ended stick as talk about truth being all-inclusive.

So where does that leave us? We must not be surprised at truth's claims, but we must test them before we believe them. If the test demonstrates truth, then we are morally compelled to believe it. And this is precisely the point from which many are trying to run. As G. K. Chesterton said, "The Christian ideal has not been tried and found wanting. It has been found difficult; and left untried."[1]

Jesus said definitively, "I am the way and the truth and the life. No one comes to the Father except through me" (John 14:6). Apply the tests of truth to the person and the message of Jesus Christ. You see not only His exclusivity, but also His uniqueness.

REFLECTION QUESTIONS

1. Why must truth be exclusive?
2. How does understanding that every worldview has exclusive claims impact the way we proclaim the Christian faith?

PERSONAL APPLICATION

1. Has your life been changed by Jesus's statement, "I am the way and the truth and the life"? Consider reflecting on His words throughout this week.
2. Do you know someone who has found Christianity difficult and walked away from the faith? How might what you've read today help you reach out to this person?

4

THE PATHWAY OF PAIN

My God, my God, why have you forsaken me?
Why are you so far from saving me,
so far from my cries of anguish?
My God, I cry out by day, but you do not answer,
by night, but I find no rest.

PSALM 22:1–2

THE LOGIC OF GOD

The difficult reality of pain forms thorny questions on which volumes have been written: Why do the innocent suffer? Why do we face all these diseases? Why the suffering of millions because of natural disasters or the tyranny of demagogues? I do not pretend to have the answers, but one thing I know: pain is a universal fact of life. Likewise, there are moral dimensions in the way we phrase our questions concerning pain, and every religion explicitly or implicitly attempts to explain pain.

But why do we even ask these questions about suffering within the context of morality? Why have we blended the fact of physical pain with the demand for a moral explanation? Who decided that pain is immoral? Indeed, almost every atheist or skeptic you read names this as the main reason for his or her denial of God's existence.

In the Judeo-Christian framework, pain is connected to the reality of evil and to the choices made by humanity at the beginning of time. The problem of pain and the problem of evil are inextricably bound. So when we assume evil, we assume good. When we assume good, we assume a moral law. And when we assume a moral law, we assume a moral Lawgiver.

You may ask, *Why does assuming a moral law necessitate a moral Lawgiver?* One reason is that because every time the question of evil is raised, it is either by a person or about a person—and that implicitly assumes that the question is a worthy one. But it is a worthy question only if people have intrinsic worth, and the only reason people have intrinsic worth is that they are the creations of One who is of ultimate worth. That person is God. So the question self-destructs for the naturalist or the pantheist. The question of the morality of evil or pain is valid only for a theist.

Furthermore, only in Christian theism is love preexistent within the Trinity, which means that love precedes human life and becomes the absolute value for us. This absolute is ultimately found only in God, and in knowing and loving God we work our way through the struggles of pain, knowing of its ultimate connection to evil and its ultimate destruction by the One who is all-good and all-loving. Indeed, God has given us the very basis for the words *good* and *love* both in concept and in language.

Not far from my home lives a young woman who was born with a very rare disease called CIPA, congenital insensitivity to pain with anhidrosis. Imagine having a body that looks normal and acts normally, except for one thing: it cannot feel physical pain. That sounds as if it would be a blessing. But the reason it's a problem is that she lives under the constant threat of injuring herself without knowing it. If she steps on a rusty nail that could infect her bloodstream, she wouldn't even realize it by sensation. If she placed her hand on a burning stove, she would not know she had just burned her hand except by looking at it. She needs constant vigilance because she could sustain an injury that could take her life or cause serious debilitation. When her family was interviewed some years ago, the line I most remember is the closing statement by her mother. She said, "I pray every night for my daughter, that God would give her a sense of pain."

If that statement were read in a vacuum, we would wonder what sort of mother she is. But because more than anyone else she understands the risks of this strange disease, there is no greater prayer she can pray than that her daughter feel pain and be able to recognize what it portends.

I ask you this simple question: If, in our finitude, we can appreciate the value of pain in even one single life, is it that difficult to grant the possibility that an infinite God can use pain to point us to a greater malady? We see through a glass darkly because all we want is to be comfortable. We cannot understand the great plan of an all-knowing God who brings us near through pain or in disappointment with pleasure.

Although we wish to avoid it, the pathway of pain can be the means to recognizing our own finitude and the rescuing grace of a God so longing to reach us that He was willing to suffer pain Himself. "My God, my God, why have you forsaken me?" was Jesus' very cry as He endured the cross for you and me. His life, death, and resurrection point to the life-defining reality that our present sorrow is only a punctuation mark because eternity with Him awaits.

Yes, intellectual answers to the problem of pain are important. But intellect alone cannot help us navigate the minefield of pain and suffering. Other worldviews may offer intellectual answers. Christianity alone offers us a *person*.

REFLECTION QUESTIONS

1. Why does the fact of a moral law necessitate a moral Lawgiver (God)?
2. Consider how the doctrine of the Trinity, God existing in a loving relationship before the creation of life, uniquely addresses the problem of pain.

PERSONAL APPLICATION

1. Has suffering been a roadblock for you or someone you know to receiving God's love? How might the cross bring comfort and hope?
2. Can you think of a time when pain was a pathway to joy or blessing in your life?

BATTLE OF THE HEART

Pilate . . . summoned Jesus and asked
him, "Are you the king of the Jews?"
"Is that your own idea," Jesus asked, "or did
others talk to you about me? . . . My kingdom is
not of this world." . . .
"You are a king, then!" said Pilate.
Jesus answered, "You say that I am a king. In
fact, the reason I was born and came into the
world is to testify to the truth. Everyone on the
side of truth listens to me."
"What is truth?" retorted Pilate.

JOHN 18:33–34, 36–38

The first and most important step to understanding the nature of truth is exemplified in a conversation between Jesus and Pilate. The conversation began with Pilate asking Jesus if indeed He was a king. The very surprising answer of Jesus was, "Are you asking this on your own, or has someone else set you up for this?"

In effect, Jesus was asking Pilate if this was a genuine question or purely an academic one. He was not merely checking on Pilate's sincerity. He was opening up Pilate's heart to himself, to reveal to Pilate his unwillingness to deal with the implications of Jesus' answer. In the pursuit of truth, *intent* is prior to content, or to the availability of it. The love of truth and the willingness to submit to its demands is the first step.

But second, Jesus said something even more extraordinary. After claiming His lordship was rooted in a kingdom that was not of this world, He said, "Everyone on the side of truth listens to me." Jesus was not merely establishing the existence of truth; He was affirming His pristine embodiment of it. He was and is identical with the truth. This means that everything He said and did, and the life He lived in the flesh, represented that which was in keeping with ultimate reality. And therefore to reject Him is to choose to govern oneself with a lie.

God's answers to life's questions are not just proven by the process of abstract reasoning; they are also sustained by the rigors of experience. And in the reality of history, God has demonstrated empirically the living out of truth in the birth, life, death, and resurrection of His Son.

In short, the intimations of truth come in multisensory fashion. God as guardian of reason leads us to check the correspondence of His Word with reality and to ascertain the coherence of the assertions. But our experience in life proves those truths in concrete reality. Our grand privilege is to know God and to bring our lives into conformity with truth, which leads us to that coherence within.

Jesus said, "If you hold to my teaching, you are really my disciples. Then you will know the truth, and the truth will set you free" (John 8:31–32). In a world increasingly enslaved by error and addiction and seduced by ideas and images to believe a lie, how wonderful to be freed by the truth of Christ's peace. The Scriptures tell us that the enemy of our souls is the father of all lies. He will do anything to keep us from coming to the truth, because it is the most valuable thing in the world and leads us to the Source of all truth, to God alone.

To all of this the skeptic might say that such conclusions may be drawn only if the God of the Bible exists. To that I heartily answer, *Absolutely!* And on numerous campuses around the world it has been my thrilling privilege to present a defense for the existence of God, the reality of the resurrection, and the authority of the Scriptures unique in their splendor and convincing in the truth they proclaim. But let us not miss what the skeptic unwittingly surrenders by saying that all this could be true only if God exists. Implicit in that concession is the law of noncontradiction and the law of rational inference, which exist only if truth exists. Truth, in turn, can exist only if there is an objective standard by which to measure it. That objective, unchanging absolute is God, further revealed to us in the person of Christ.

Growing up in India, I heard a story of a little boy who had lots of pretty marbles. But he was constantly eyeing his sister's bagful of candy. One day he said to her, "If you give me all your candy, I'll give you all of my marbles." She gave it much thought and agreed to the trade. He took all her candy and went back to his room to get his marbles. But the more he admired them, the more reluctant he became to give them all up. So he hid the best of them under his pillow and took the rest to her. That night, she slept soundly, while he tossed and turned restlessly, unable to sleep and thinking, *I wonder if she gave me all the candy?*

I have often wondered, when I see our angry culture claiming that God has not given us enough evidence, if it is not the veiled restlessness of people who live in doubt because of their own duplicity. The battle in our time is posed as one of the intellect, in the assertion that truth is unknowable. But that may be only a veneer for the real battle: the battle of the heart, which Christ alone is able to transform.

REFLECTION QUESTIONS

1. What is the first and most important step to understanding the nature of truth?
2. Why does truth demand an objective standard?

PERSONAL APPLICATION

1. Jesus said, "If you hold to my teaching, you are really my disciples." How will His words change your life and witness this week?
2. Can you think of a time when, like the little boy with the marbles, you withheld your best from God and wondered if He was giving you His best?

CHRISTIANITY WITHOUT CHRIST?

God was pleased to have all his fullness
dwell in him, and through him to reconcile
to himself all things, whether things on
earth or things in heaven, by making peace
through his blood, shed on the cross.

COLOSSIANS 1:19–20

aul Tillich, the noted existentialist theologian, traveled to Asia years ago to hold conferences with various Buddhist thinkers. He was studying the significance of religious leaders to the movements they had engendered. Tillich reportedly asked what if, by some fluke, the Buddha had never lived and turned out to be some sort of fabrication? What would be the implications for Buddhism? Mind you, I would conclude that Tillich was concerned with the indispensability of the Buddha—not his authenticity.

The scholars did not hesitate to answer. If the Buddha was a myth, they said, it did not matter at all. Why? Because Buddhism should be judged as an abstract philosophy—as a system of living. Whether its concepts originated with the Buddha is irrelevant. As an aside, I think the Buddha himself would have concurred. Knowing that his death was imminent, he beseeched his followers not to focus on him but to remember his teachings. Not his life but his way of life was to be attended to and propagated.

So, what of other world religions? Hinduism, as a conglomeration of thinkers and philosophies and gods, can certainly do without many of its deities. Some other major religions face the same predicament.

Is Christianity similar? Could God the Father have sent another instead of Jesus? I say to you that the answer is most categorically *No.* Jesus did not merely claim to be a prophet in a continuum of prophets. He is the unique Son of God, part of the very Godhead that Christianity calls the Trinity.

The apostle Paul wrote:

The Son is the image of the invisible God, the firstborn over all creation. For in him all things were created: things in heaven and on earth, visible and invisible, whether thrones or powers or rulers or authorities; all things have been created through him and for him. He is before all things, and in him all things hold together. And he is the head of the body, the church; he is the beginning and the firstborn from among the dead, so that in everything he might have the supremacy. (Colossians 1:15–18)

Moreover, Jesus Himself prayed just hours before He was to be crucified,

"Father, the hour has come. Glorify your Son, that your Son may glorify you. For you granted him authority over all people that he might give eternal life to all those you have given him. Now this is eternal life: that they know you, the only true God, and Jesus Christ, whom you have sent." (John 17:1–3)

Jesus is absolutely indispensable to Christianity—and His claims are also unique. First is His description of the human condition. He declared that the heart is in rebellion against God.

Second, Jesus offers a unique solution to the problem. The provision He gives for you and me is utterly unique, and it is not cheap.

It is the cross. This graciousness of forgiveness is not found in other worldviews. For instance, Islam says that for you to get to heaven, your good deeds will have to outweigh your bad. In other words, you pay.

When Christ comes and says to you and me that He is offering forgiveness and doing so through the payment of His life on the cross, it is an extraordinary truth. The Bible says we need a Savior and we need forgiveness. There is only one place in the world where love, forgiveness, and justice come together, and that is at the cross. This truth of Christ's grace is unique.

Third, Jesus is unique because in Him was no sin; He lived a perfect life. Even Pontius Pilate declared, "I find no fault in this man" (Luke 23:4 KJV).

And fourth, His resurrection is the ultimate demonstration of His uniqueness.

Christianity, therefore, *is* Christ. Indeed, Englishman John Stott wrote, "If Jesus was not God in human flesh, Christianity is exploded. We are left with just another religion with some beautiful ideas and noble ethics; its unique distinction has gone."[1]

At the very heart of Christianity, Jesus is the image and the incarnation of the invisible God—the One who came to live among us to show us God's love, perfection, and grace. And this reality changes everything.

REFLECTION QUESTIONS

1. Why is the belief that Jesus is the unique Son of God a nonnegotiable in the Christian worldview?
2. How are Jesus' description of the human condition and His solution utterly unique?

PERSONAL APPLICATION

1. Jesus "changes everything." How might this truth change your life today?
2. Jesus offers us God's grace and forgiveness and calls us to extend His kindness to others. Whom could you reach out to with God's love and forgiveness?

7

LOSING SIGHT

You also were included in Christ when you heard the message of truth, the gospel of your salvation. When you believed, you were marked in him with a seal, the promised Holy Spirit, who is a deposit guaranteeing our inheritance until the redemption of those who are God's possession—to the praise of his glory.

EPHESIANS 1:13–14

Years ago, my family and I were visiting the city of Bedford, England. In the heart of Bedford stands a larger-than-life statue of the famed seventeenth-century author John Bunyan. In fact, so imposing is the size of that sculpture that someone had painted bold, gigantic white footsteps from the edifice all the way to the public toilets. The message implied, sarcastically or otherwise, that Bunyan still lives.

Any reader of literature knows that though Bunyan has long been dead, his brilliant work, *The Pilgrim's Progress*, does indeed live on. That book has been translated into more languages than most other books in history, with the exception of the Bible.

So my family and I wandered through the museum built to his memory, where there was exhibited a copy of the book in every language in which it had been printed. We were quite impressed by the people of various nationalities engrossed in the display, walking from room to room, studying the exhibits.

As I was leaving, I commented to the woman at the front desk, "Isn't it amazing that a simple little book from the hands of a mender of pots and pans has won such worldwide acclaim?"

She paused and said, "I suppose that is true, but I must confess that I haven't read it."

If there hadn't been a hard floor beneath me, I would have voluntarily fainted. Unable to help myself, I asked her, "Why not?"

"I found it too difficult, I suppose," she replied dispassionately.

If shock were to be measured along a scale, at this point I was nearly off the chart. What does one say to the person who sells tickets to a museum, the existence of which is owed to one book, while she herself has left the work unread? I recommended that for the sake of sheer curiosity, if not propriety, she might at least try the children's version, so she could get a mild taste of what the interest was all about.

Bunyan's classic tale is a shrewd and an insightful allegory of the journey of life. Christian, the lead character who represents each of us as pilgrims, struggles with a heavy burden. He encounters the testing of Vanity Fair, the Slough of Despond, and so on. It is only when Christian reaches the foot of the cross at the top of the hill that his burden falls off him.

But the journey doesn't end there. Bunyan writes,

Then he stood still for a while to look with wonder and amazement; for it was so surprising to him that the sight of the Cross should accomplish the release of his burden. Therefore he looked again and again, even until inward springs of water flowed down his cheeks. Now as he stood looking and weeping, behold three Shining Ones approached and saluted him with the benediction, "Let peace be upon you."

So the first Shining One said to him, "Your sins have been forgiven." The second stripped Christian of his rags and clothed him with a complete change of garment. The third set a mark upon his forehead and gave him a scroll with a seal on it, which he directed should be looked at as he ran and handed in upon arrival at the gate of the Celestial City.

The first angel meets his spiritual need, the second addresses his physical needs, and the third engages his intellectual needs with a map to guide and instruct him along the journey. The Christian's walk involves all three areas of life: the spiritual, the practical, and the intellectual. These are not mutually exclusive.

Yet, like the employee in the Bedford museum who had not read the work responsible for the museum's very existence, we may disregard the very Author of our lives. This is true not only of skeptics but of confessing believers and followers of Christ as well. How easy it is to lose sight and disregard the great inheritance promised through the gospel: God's own Spirit within us.

So, may we hold fast daily to His Word and His Spirit's indelible mark upon on us at the foot of the cross as His dearly loved children! God's Word and His indwelling presence are given to us to inform, enrich, teach, correct, and guide us to the "Celestial City." If we lose sight of these realities, we have lost the light that guides us on the journey, whether it is through the valley or around a hope-filled bend.

But oh, too, rejoice in the tenderness of God's gifts to us! He is complete, and thus are we, in what He gives to you and me: He forgives us. He robes us. And He guides us home—with the seal of His very Spirit upon us, both now and when we arrive to meet Him face-to-face.

REFLECTION QUESTIONS

1. When does Christian's burden fall off of him, and where might you find an example of this in the Bible?
2. What three gifts is Christian given, and how do they apply to the journey of faith?

PERSONAL APPLICATION

1. The Christian walk involves the spiritual, the practical, and the intellectual. Take an inventory of your life. Where are you most in need of God's direction and indwelling presence?
2. Consider someone you've been trying to reach with the gospel. Of these three areas, what is his or her most pressing need, and how could you address it?

8

THE GREATEST INVESTMENT

Two of them were going to a village called
Emmaus, about seven miles from Jerusalem.
They were talking with each other about
everything that had happened. As they talked
and discussed these things with each other,
Jesus himself came up and walked along with
them; but they were kept from recognizing him.

I once visited the State Hermitage Museum in Saint Petersburg, Russia, with my wife and my son. My wife, formally trained as a nurse, is a student of the fine arts. She studies every little thing while I do most things in a hurry so we can get to our next destination. As we walked through the museum, she studied every painting while I glanced here and there. I recall it being a magnificent and historic place, but not much more.

Some years later I was reading a book by Henri Nouwen. He was teaching at Harvard and had just returned from an exhausting trip of lecturing when he encountered a poster he had never seen before. Two years later he resigned from his teaching post and went to the State Hermitage Museum to find one painting: the one represented in the poster that he couldn't get out of his mind. It was *The Return of the Prodigal Son*, Rembrandt's depiction of the prodigal son coming home. Nouwen traveled to Russia and sat in front of that painting for four hours—and it changed his life. After this encounter, he knew that he wanted to work with mentally handicapped children and joined a community in Toronto dedicated to this ministry.

Sadly, when I saw the painting, I paused for a few fleeting moments, then moved on to the next. I have lived to regret that loss.

One of my favorite authors, A. W. Tozer, once observed:

I have often wished that there were some way to bring modern Christians into a deeper spiritual life painlessly by short easy lessons; but such wishes are vain. No shortcuts exist! . . . May not the inadequacy of much of our spiritual experience be traced back to our habit of skipping through the corridors of the kingdom like little children through the marketplace, chattering about everything but pausing to learn the true value of nothing?[1]

I went through the museum, as Tozer mused, skipping through the corridors, looking at everything but pausing to learn the true value of nothing.

May I remind you how easy it is to do this, even as we are seeking after God? Remember Jesus' disciples in the closing chapter of Luke's gospel? They were disillusioned, confused, and fearful. On the Sunday following Jesus' crucifixion, two of them were walking to a village called Emmaus, about seven miles from Jerusalem. They were talking about everything that had happened the previous week when Jesus Himself appeared and walked along with them. But somehow they were kept from recognizing Him. Jesus asked them why they were so downcast, and they responded by asking Him if He was the only visitor to Jerusalem who didn't know what had happened there over the weekend.

The delightful irony of their question is that *He* was the only one who *did* know what had happened! Luke tells us, "And beginning with Moses and all the Prophets, he explained to them what was said in all the Scriptures concerning himself" (Luke 24:27).

The seven miles flew by and before they realized it, they arrived in Emmaus. True easterners, the two disciples invited Jesus to join them for dinner. As they sat down to eat, Jesus became the host and took the bread in His hands and blessed it. Suddenly, the disciples were stopped in their tracks and they recognized Him: *Jesus!* Whether when He broke the bread they were reminded of a meal shared with Him previously, or when they caught a glimpse of the wounds in His hands, their eyes were opened to Him. Though they had spent a couple of hours journeying seven miles with Jesus, they did not pause to take in the weight of all He shared with them until they were seated before Him.

Contrast them with a surgeon at work, completely focused on the delicate task at hand and the patient entrusted to his or her care. Think too of the hours one must invest in preparing for such a vocation and the disciplines needed in order to develop such skills. Or consider a mother with her children. Think of the hours she has invested to be by their sides and to understand what they really need.

Can we do any less in the discipline of study and preparation to finish the task to which God has called us? To echo Charles Spurgeon, the study of God is the highest science, the loftiest pursuit, and the mightiest discipline. Its rewards are immeasurable: "Blessed are those who keep his statutes and seek him with all their heart. . . . Great peace have those who love your law, and nothing can make them stumble" (Psalm 119:2, 165). Tozer concluded, "God has not bowed to our nervous haste nor embraced the methods of our machine age. It is well that we accept the hard truth now: the man who would know God must give time to Him!"[2]

Might we sit still long enough to take in what God has for us? That is the greatest investment we will ever make.

REFLECTION QUESTIONS

1. Why do you think, as Luke records, that the two men traveling to Emmaus with Jesus were kept from recognizing Him?
2. In what way does A. W. Tozer describe the deeper spiritual life? How does it compare to a surgeon's work?

PERSONAL APPLICATION

1. The frenetic pace of our world can lead us to "nervous haste." What can you do today to invest in eternal matters and relationships?
2. Blessed are those who seek God with their whole hearts, wrote the psalmist. What blessings have you known or would you hope to experience in spending time with God?

SHUTTING THE GATE

You were taught, with regard to your former way of life, to put off your old self, which is being corrupted by its deceitful desires; to be made new in the attitude of your minds; and to put on the new self, created to be like God in true righteousness and holiness.

EPHESIANS 4:22-24

I was speaking in a country some years ago where I was introduced to a man who had a daily habit of taking his little boy up a hill. The man would point over the border and tell his son, "Your duty in life is to kill as many of them on the other side as you can."

Even today it is hard for me to comprehend this. Sadly, this man could never shut the gate on the past. And so he dragged the heavy carcass of historical prejudice and draped that corpse over the shoulders of the next generation as a reminder to continue the carnage.

Lamentably, we discover the seeds of hate and separation in the opening pages of Scripture and within the very first family. Incredibly, the first murder in the Bible did not occur because of two irreconcilable political theories. The murder of a man by his own brother was an act unmistakably borne out of their differing responses to God! Trapped by the temporal, Cain was deluded by the belief that he could vanquish spiritual reality with brute force. God saw the inevitable result of the jealousy and hatred deep within Cain's heart, and in a challenge that would determine his destiny, warned him to deal with it. "If you do what is right, will you not be accepted? But if you do not do what is right, sin is crouching at the door; it desires to have you, but you must rule over it" (Genesis 4:7).

Tragically, Cain ignored God's words, and taking matters into his own hands, he killed his brother Abel.

As extreme as these life experiences may sound, who of us has not struggled with anger, forgiveness, and pride? Yet we are called as followers of Christ to love our neighbors as ourselves and to "be kind to one another, tenderhearted, forgiving one another, as God in Christ forgave you" (Ephesians 4:32 ESV). Why? Because Scripture tells us that every life is valuable to God: "You created my inmost being; you knit me together in my mother's womb," uttered the psalmist David. "I praise you because I am fearfully and wonderfully made" (Psalm 139:13–14).

At its core life is sacred and of inestimable value, whether it is the life of a darling child in the fresh blossom of childhood, or the life of an elderly, weak, and frail recluse. We are each made in God's sacred image. Think of this truth! That is why murder is described in Scripture for what it is: an attack upon God's image. That is also why we are told, "Everyone who hates his brother is a murderer" (1 John 3:15 ESV). Murder and even hateful words are attempts to destroy God's image in another and to deny one's value and spiritual essence. That essence gives us our dignity and our worth. That essence is our glory and true home.

I find it quite remarkable that Jesus did not specifically address some of the pressing social issues of His day. Rather, He went to the heart of what separates us from God and what transforms: we are sinners in need of God's cleansing forgiveness and restoration.

The truth is, we desperately need a Savior, every one of us, whatever our past and whatever our present. We need a God who not only changes what we do, but what we want to do. Scripture declares that we are "made new in the attitude of [our] minds . . . created to be like God in true righteousness and holiness" (Ephesians 4:23–24). What a hope and what a promise!

No longer are we bound by chains of the past, never to shut the gate on hate and unforgiveness. Rather, if we are in Christ we are filled with God's Spirit, and "the fruit of the Spirit is love, joy, peace, patience, kindness, goodness, faithfulness, gentleness, self-control" (Galatians 5:22–23 ESV). May we bear witness to God's love and forgiveness this day.

REFLECTION QUESTIONS

1. How did Cain's misunderstanding of God provoke him to kill his brother?
2. Why does the Bible equate hate with murder, and how does Jesus' emphasis on the heart speak to pressing social issues today?

PERSONAL APPLICATION

1. What steps have you taken or could you take to shut the gate to unforgiveness and hate?
2. "We need a God who not only changes what we do, but what we want to do." Take time to seek God's guidance, help, and restoration in your desires.

10

CHASING SHADOWS

"Which is easier: to say, 'Your sins are
forgiven,' or to say, 'Get up and walk'? But
I want you to know that the Son of Man
has authority on earth to forgive sins." So
he said to the paralyzed man, "I tell you,
get up, take your mat and go home."
Immediately he stood up in front of them,
took what he had been lying on and went
home praising God.

LUKE 5:23–25

In an interesting encounter between Jesus and the paralytic, we see a defining reminder of the relationship between soul and body, the temporal and the eternal (Luke 5:17–26). The friends of this paralyzed man did everything they could to bring him within the sight and touch of Jesus. They even disfigured the property of the person in whose house Jesus was visiting in the hope that He would perform a miracle for their friend. They must have reasoned that if Jesus could make a paralyzed man walk again, replacing a roof would be a minor problem. But as they lowered this man within reach of Jesus, they were not expecting an apologetics discussion.

"Which of the two is harder," asked Jesus, "to bring physical healing or to forgive a person's sins?" The irresistible answer was self-evident, was it not? To bring physical healing is harder because that would be such a miraculous thing, visible to the naked eye. The invisible act of forgiveness had far less evidentiary value.

Yet, as they pondered and as we ponder, we discover repeatedly in life that the way God works is so different from the way we expect. We move from the material to the spiritual in terms of the spectacular, but God moves from the spiritual to the material in terms of the essential. The physical is the concrete external—a shadow comparatively. The spiritual is the intangible internal—the objective actuality.

Rather than chasing truth, we often chase shadows. We chase them because they are a haunting enticement of the substance without being the substance themselves. It takes a jolt, sometimes even a painful jolt, to remind us where reality lies and where shadows seduce.

Jesus was so aware of this weakness within us that He often walked the second mile to meet us, in order that something more dramatic might be used to put into perspective for us what is of greater importance to God.

Yes, He did heal that man, but not without the reminder of what the ultimate miracle was. Once we understand this, we understand the relationship between touching the soul and touching the body. Here Jesus followed the act of forgiveness with the easier act of physical healing. If the paralytic was a wise man, he would walk with the awareness that the apparently less-visible miracle was actually more miraculous than the more visible one—even as his feeling of gratitude for his restored body would remain a constant reminder to him of the restoration of his soul.

As I have pondered this and the many other examples of Jesus' acts of mercy, I look at our hurting world that is desensitized to the gospel message—the message that cleanses the soul, heals the inner being, and brings light to the body. Our world is weighed down with pain, fear, suffering, and poverty. Our world is so broken that if we were to stare reality in the face, we would wish it really were only a shadow and not an actual embodiment. Such is the blind eye people turn to the familiar and dismiss as mere shadows what is tragically real. Sadly, both body and soul are forgotten in the process. The cost in human suffering is beyond computation.

In such a world, the question becomes: Does Jesus still lift body and soul out of the shadow and bring it into the light? I believe He does, and what an answer is the cross upon which "he has borne our griefs and carried our sorrows" (Isaiah 53:4 ESV). Such is the power of love. It is Christ who shows that unless a person's pain is understood, one will never understand a person's soul. He Himself is the best reminder of the reward of chasing truth versus chasing shadows.

REFLECTION QUESTIONS

1. Read the story of paralyzed man in Luke 5:17–26. What do his friends' actions suggest about their estimate of this man and Jesus?
2. Why is forgiveness rather than healing the ultimate miracle? Why is the physical a shadow compared to the soul?

PERSONAL APPLICATION

1. Can you recall an instance when you made a great effort to introduce a person to Jesus? How could you model the compassion and persistence of the friends in today's Scripture for someone you know?
2. Rather than chasing truth, we often chase shadows. Where has chasing shadows led you? What about chasing truth?

11

CROSSING BRIDGES

Paul then stood up in the meeting of the
Areopagus and said: "People of Athens! I see
that in every way you are very religious. . . .
As some of your own poets have said, 'We
are his offspring.' Therefore since we are
God's offspring, we should not think that the
divine being is like gold or silver or stone—
an image made by human design and skill."

ACTS 17:22, 28–29

The weighty differences of worldviews can separate us from others, but in my work of offering a defense of the Christian faith, I know firsthand they can be discussed without compromise and without animosity, with gentleness and respect.

Being raised in the East and living in the West, I have learned that reason and rationalizing are not the same thing. People often think they have *reasons* for their belief. But that very word means different ideas to different people. To a professor of philosophy, *reason* may mean a sound argument. To a teacher in a high school in India, *reason* may mean cultural respect for one's own ancestral beliefs. It is critically important to know that behind every belief is a believer, and behind every question is a questioner. The belief is part of the worldview, and the worldview is not always well scrutinized by reason.

So here again is what I present as a coherent worldview. Whether religious or irreligious, everyone has a worldview. A worldview basically offers answers to four necessary questions: origin, meaning, morality, and destiny. In our very human longing for answers to these questions we share common ground. That worldview must answer individual questions in correspondence to reality, and the sum of all the answers must be coherent.

As I observe the apostle Paul, who was cradled within three cultures (Jewish, Greek, and Roman), I see how he approached his mixed audience. A look at his assumptions and his method is very instructive. His address to the Athenians in Acts 17 gives me the blueprint. We are told, for starters, how he was "greatly distressed to see that the city was full of idols" (v. 16). This holy anxiety is an indispensable prerequisite to significant communication and crossing bridges.

So, first, *you will never lighten any load until you feel the pressure in your own soul.* That distress led Paul to observe and listen, to dialogue, reason, discuss, and persuade many through the power of the Holy Spirit. Listening is a vital part of responding. The more and the better we hear others, the more and the better they will hear us. This is especially true today when sensitivities run so deep.

There is a second assumption Paul makes: *a rigorous religion can be conceived and nurtured in ignorance by the masses.* Paul communicated that the Athenians' yearning for the divine was a positive trait, but their systems of worship were not good enough if their truths were not tested. He applauded their search for God. That positive lead-in is commendable. It is self-defeating to trample underfoot everything others hold dear before giving them the message of Christ. My mother used to say, "There is no point cutting off a person's nose and then giving them a rose to smell." Cultures carry huge connections to the past. Respect must be given, but the driving point must always be toward the truth. Gently present the gap between what is believed and what is true.

Maintaining sensitivity, Paul also capitalized on his listeners' lack of understanding of their own beliefs. One of the most shocking lessons one learns in countries where culture is interwoven with religion is that living within a certain framework all the time is, in a sense, the surest way to be detached from it. A Chinese proverb says, "If you want to know what water is, don't ask the fish."

Most Hindus know little about Hinduism's scriptures or its development in dogma. Most Buddhists know little about Buddhism. Religion is much more a culture to most people than it is a carefully thought-through system of truth. Even Islam finds the same ignorance. Dare I say most Christians know very little about the teaching and history of their own beliefs.

Paul had before him "seekers after God," but they were scanty in their understanding of truth. How did he meet the challenge? It was his allusion to one of their poets that stuck and helped him find that soft reach and a legitimate bridge.

We must direct people in such a way as to open them up within their own assumptions, moving them from what they know and believe to what they don't know and what they disbelieve. Then the conclusion is inescapable: *What I now believe may be good, but it's not good enough.* There always has to be a persuasive element, and that comes from their familiarity with some authority and the ability to identify with that.

Third, *Christianity is not a religion or perspective; it is God's self-disclosure in Christ.* It is built on and built through a relationship. Paul strove ardently to drive this point home. The crowd had gathered to hear what this "babbler" was saying (v. 18), but his message pointed—as ours must—to the person and work of Jesus Christ. The ultimate question is not "What is the answer?" It is "Who will answer?" The cry of everyone's heart is for a Savior, a Champion, a personal Redeemer. It was this Redeemer whom Paul presented.

At great personal cost, Paul took the gospel to Athens. His sensitivities, his knowledge, his finding common ground, and his presentation of the unique answers of Jesus built the framework of his message. It is little wonder that he changed history by crossing bridges with such effectiveness to the known world. It is literally and figuratively true that he used the Greek language and the Roman road. We can't do any less.

Ultimately, the change of a person's heart is God's work. And in doing our part, we must ever rest in that conviction.

REFLECTION QUESTIONS

1. What three things did the apostle Paul do in Athens to cross bridges and engage in conversation for the gospel?
2. Read Acts 17:22–34. Why do you think Paul's appeal to being God's offspring is so effective?

PERSONAL APPLICATION

1. How might the idea that "you will never lighten any load until you feel the pressure in your own soul" affect the way you pray and interact with others this week?
2. Many Christians know very little about the teaching and history of their own beliefs. Consider reading through one of Paul's letters or even the book of Acts to dig deeper into God's Word.

12

A ROYAL WEDDING
JUST LIKE MINE

See what great love the Father has lavished
on us, that we should be called children
of God! And that is what we are! . . .
This is how we know what love is: Jesus Christ
laid down his life for us. And we ought to lay
down our lives for our brothers and sisters.

1 JOHN 3:1, 16

Well, the world has another princess. Millions watched as Harry wed Meghan and tied the royal knot. Unfortunately, I was in the thick of travel so couldn't watch it live. But as I sit at the Bangkok airport en route to Singapore, I am watching the highlights. There's no escape—every television is showing the wedding.

As I watched, I marveled at how similar this was to my wedding in May, forty-six years ago.

Harry married Meghan. Her shorter name is Meg. My wife's full name is Margaret—shorter version, Meg or Margie. They were married in Windsor Castle. I was married 240 miles away from Windsor, Ontario—same name, same city referenced. She has now become a princess. My wife, Margie, went to school in Toronto on Princess Avenue. Meghan is a beautiful blend of two races. My Margie is a beautiful blend of the Irish and Scottish. What's more, we have added to that splendid coalescence with three beautiful offspring.

Harry is a prince and the second son of Charles. I was the second son of my father and my middle name, Kumar, means *Prince*. Harry was congratulated by his grandfather, the Duke of Edinburgh. When the duke visited India about six decades ago, he shook hands with my younger brother and congratulated him for being the youngest member of the choir. Later my younger brother shook hands with me. On second thought, the duke may not have shaken hands with my brother, but he certainly greeted him. And then my brother greeted me—same thing.

They were treated to a fiery message by a minister whose last name was Curry. After our wedding rehearsal we enjoyed curry for our dinner treat that night, which was just as fiery. Our reception was at Howard Johnson's. Knowing the English, I am sure at least one of the cooks would have been a Howard or a Johnson.

They rode away in a horse-drawn carriage loaned by Harry's father. We drove away in our 1972 Plymouth Duster, given by my parents. Interestingly, Duster is the name of Banner-General Tylee Khirgan's warhorse. Of course, just as in this story, we could have driven away in a limousine.

Yes, sadly, there were some differences. There was a garbage strike in Toronto for the weeks preceding our wedding, and the only place where there was no garbage piled up was near the airport. So all of our photographs were with the airport in the background. How prophetic was that about our future? Apart from this minor difference, you can see the incredible similarities, can't you?

All jesting aside, don't be deceived by the flutter of the heart. Love is a commitment that will be tested in the most vulnerable areas of spirituality, a commitment that will force you to make some very difficult choices. It is a commitment that demands that you deal with your lust, your greed, your pride, your power, your desire to control, your temper, your patience, and every area of temptation that the Bible so clearly talks about. It demands the quality of commitment that Jesus demonstrates in His relationship to us: "God demonstrates his own love for us in this: While we were still sinners, Christ died for us" (Romans 5:8).

In reality, every wedding properly viewed and respected is a fairy-tale wedding. Two little ones born worlds apart meet, and the hearts join to make those two lives one. Under God and in Christ we are all children of royalty and ought to celebrate that treasured position. Living with that blessing and serving the King of kings is our joy. Marriage and the home are God's treasured gifts, and we ought to see them the way God does.

It is not accidental that the first miracle our Lord performed was at a wedding. Behind the celebratory intake of food is the miracle of two lives becoming one and surrendering themselves to each other. A heart surrendering to Christ is a miracle. Two hearts becoming one under Christ is a double miracle. Our homes may not be palaces, but every home is a palace when the King of kings indwells the hearts of those who cherish each other as God designed them to do.

The father of the new princess spoke touching words from a distance: "My baby looks beautiful." To him she will always be "my baby." How much more our Abba Father beams with His love when two of His children honor each other because they honor Him. He probably says, "My kids." They are forever His children.

Our wedding and the royal wedding had no similarities in grandeur or status, and rightly so, but they did have the most important one: love triumphed and found its destiny. They looked lovely and happy. May that beauty and joy last their lifetimes.

Moreover, may you know the depth of love that God alone, the King of kings, offers to you this very moment. Under His banner of love and through Christ's costly sacrifice we can live as children of royalty, greatly loved. Now that is a love worth celebrating!

REFLECTION QUESTIONS

1. What is true love according to 1 John 3?
2. What does Romans 5:8 say about the human condition and Christ's response to us?

PERSONAL APPLICATION

1. "Love is a commitment that will be tested in the most vulnerable areas." Pray through the promises of Scripture and ask God to meet you in your areas of need.
2. How does the assurance that in Christ you are a daughter or son of the King of kings inspire you?

13

EVERY THREAD MATTERS

The Spirit helps us in our weakness. We do not
know what we ought to pray for, but the Spirit
himself intercedes for us through wordless
groans. And he who searches our hearts
knows the mind of the Spirit, because the Spirit
intercedes for God's people in accordance with
the will of God. And we know that in all things
God works for the good of those who love him,
who have been called according to his purpose.

ROMANS 8:26–28

I struggled as a teenager growing up in Delhi. For those of you who have read my story in *Walking from East to West* (Zondervan, 2006), you know failure was writ large on my life. My dad basically looked at me and said, "You're going to be a huge embarrassment to the family—one failure after another." And he was right, given the way I was headed. I wanted to get out of everything I was setting my hand to, and I lacked discipline.

During this time, India was at war and the Defence Academy was looking for general duties pilots to be trained. So I applied and I went to be interviewed, which involved an overnight train journey from the city of Delhi. It was wintertime and we were outside freezing for about five days as we went through physical endurance and other tests. There were three hundred applicants; they were going to select ten. On the last day they put their selection of names out on the board, and I was positioned number three.

I phoned my family and said, "You aren't going to believe this. I'm going to make it. I'm number three. The only thing that's left is the interview. The psychological testing is tomorrow, and I'll be home."

The next morning, I began my interview with the chief commanding officer, who looked to me like Churchill sitting across the table. He asked me question after question. Then he said, "Son, I'm going to break your heart today." He continued, "I'm going to reject you. I'm not going to pass you in this test."

"May I ask you why, sir?" I replied.

"Yes. Psychologically, you're not wired to kill. And this job is about killing."

I felt that I was on the verge of wanting to prove him wrong—but I knew better, both for moral reasons and for his size! I went back to my room and didn't talk to anybody. I packed my bags, got into the train, and arrived in Delhi. My parents and friends were waiting at the platform with garlands and sweets in their hands to congratulate me. No one knew. I thought to myself, *How do I even handle this? Where do I even begin?* They were celebrating, and yet for me, it was all over.

Or so I thought.

I was to discover later that God is the Grand Weaver of our lives. Every thread matters and is there for a purpose. Had I been selected, I would have had to commit twenty years to the Indian Armed Forces. It was the very next year that my father had the opportunity to move to Canada. My brother and I moved there as the first installment, and the rest of them followed. It was there I went to business school and God redirected my path to theological training. It was there that I met my wife, Margie; there my whole life changed. The rest is history. Had I been in the Indian Air Force, who knows what thread I'd have pulled to try to wreck the fabric?

Thankfully, our disappointments matter to God, and He has a way of taking even some of the bitterest moments we go through and making them into something of great significance in our lives. It's hard to understand at the time. Not one of us says, "I can hardly wait to see where this thread is going to fit." Rather, we say, "This is not the pattern I want."

Yet one day the Shepherd of our souls will put it all together—and give us an eternity to revel in the marvel of what God has done. Our Father holds the threads of the design, and I'm so immensely grateful that He is the Grand Weaver.

REFLECTION QUESTIONS

1. According to Romans 8, what is the role of the Holy Spirit in the life of the Christian?
2. What does it mean that God is the Grand Weaver of our lives? Do you believe this?

PERSONAL APPLICATION

1. Have disappointments moved you toward God or away from Him? Where do you see God at work in your life today?
2. God declares that "the Spirit helps us in our weakness," interceding on our behalf. Invite the Holy Spirit to be your Counselor, Comforter, and Advocate and to pray for you and your concerns.

THE HEART OF GOD

"The Israelites will be like the sand on the seashore, which cannot be measured or counted. In the place where it was said to them, 'You are not my people,' they will be called 'children of the living God.'"

HOSEA 1:10

believe one of the most profound poems ever written was penned by an Englishman named Francis Thompson. Thompson was a genius, but he became a drug addict and was on the run for many years. Toward the later part of his life he wrote the magnificent masterpiece he called "The Hound of Heaven." The poem describes God as the persistent Hound who, with loving feet, follows and follows until He catches up with this person who is trying to escape Him. Wrote Thompson:

> I fled Him, down the nights and down the days;
> I fled Him, down the arches of the years;
> I fled Him, down the labyrinthine ways
> Of my own mind; and in the mist of tears
> I hid from Him, and under running laughter.
> Up vistaed hopes I sped;
> And shot, precipitated,
> Adown Titanic glooms of chasmed fears,
> From those strong Feet that followed, followed after.[1]

As the poem comes to an end, Thompson depicts the persistent cry of God to the one who flees His presence, the one God pursues to the end:

> "Ah, fondest, blindest, weakest,
> I am He Whom thou seekest!
> Thou dravest love from thee, who dravest Me."[2]

With the wisdom of one who had found himself chased after, Thompson noted the heart of God and the contradiction of humanity. We run away, fearful that if we have God, we might have nothing else beside. And God says, "You were weak and blind and miserable when you were driving Me away, because you were actually driving love away from you. I am the One you seek."

We encounter a similar story in the book of Hosea. The life and ministry of the prophet Hosea is a fascinating, mystifying look at the love of God and the human tendency to push that love away and hide from it. Hosea was a prophet called by God to marry Gomer, a harlot who continually left the loving home Hosea had provided to return to her life of prostitution. One can almost hear the whispers among the people to whom Hosea faithfully preached, until someone was brave enough to ask: "Hosea, can you tell us how it is you continue to love this woman, a woman who has so betrayed you and repeatedly abandoned her commitment to you? How can a holy man of God like you be joined to a woman such as this?"

And Hosea essentially responds, "I will be delighted to answer your question if you will first answer a question of mine. How can a holy God like this love such a harlotrous people like us?"

The first thing the book of Hosea reveals over and over about the nature of God's relationship with us is that God gives to us a love we do not deserve. We do not merit it.

Second, not only is the love of God unmerited, it is also a love that grows and is sustained by relationship. Remarkably, God even utters a wedding vow, pledging His love and faithfulness: "I will betroth you to me forever; I will betroth you in righteousness and justice, in love and compassion. I will betroth you in faithfulness, and you will acknowledge the Lord" (Hosea 2:19–20). The longer we walk with God, the more we understand how much of a gift this love is.

Through the prophet Hosea, God spoke graphically to a nation running from His presence: "A spirit of prostitution is in their heart; they do not acknowledge the Lord" (5:4). Yet mercifully God chases after them, woos them into His arms, pays the price to buy them back, cleans them up, and takes them home. He declares, "I will say to those called 'Not my people,' 'You are my people'; and they will say, 'You are my God'" (2:23).

God's message through Hosea will send a deep ray of hope into our hearts if we listen carefully.

Indeed, in Christ, God makes His love plain to us. He shows us what it means to be human, removes the corruption of sin, and provides new life, hope, and meaning. God wants to see humanity flourish. Let us come to the cross as we are: children desiring love, sinners needing mercy, souls weary of running through our nights and days, and ready to follow the One who ordains us.

REFLECTION QUESTIONS

1. Take time to read through the brief book of Hosea or specifically chapters 11 and 14. Where do you see instances of God's unmerited love?
2. How does Hosea's love for his adulterous wife foreshadow Christ's love for us as sinners?

PERSONAL APPLICATION

1. The story of Hosea can send a deep ray of hope into our hearts if we listen carefully. What particular detail of this story offers you hope?
2. In Christ, God removes the corruption of sin and provides new life, hope, and meaning. Where has Christ made the most difference in your life? Where might He continue to transform you?

15

WHAT HAPPENED TO
YOUR HANDS?

A week later his disciples were in the house
again, and Thomas was with them. Though
the doors were locked, Jesus came and stood
among them and said, "Peace be with you!"
Then he said to Thomas, "Put your finger here;
see my hands. Reach out your hand and put
it into my side. Stop doubting and believe."
Thomas said to him, "My Lord and my God!"

JOHN 20:26-28

have often referenced what talk show host Larry King once said in his response to a particular question: "If you could select any one person across all of history to interview, who would it be?" Mr. King's answer was that he would like to interview Jesus Christ. When the questioner continued, "And what would you like to ask Him?" King said he would like to ask if He was indeed virgin-born because the answer would define history for him.

It is not possible to live without asking questions—and what better source for the answers than the One who claimed to be the way, the truth, and the life? If one could only be face-to-face with Him from whom life comes, how delightful would be those moments when the most confounding and painful questions of life are raised. Though unaware that they were walking with the risen Christ, the men who walked on the Emmaus Road said that their hearts burned within them as He opened up the past, the present, and the future. When they realized who He was, a light for all of history had been turned on.

In the same way, it may be that when the time comes to sit across the table from the Lord of history, the answer to the skeptic and the believer will be more visible than it will be in need of utterance. This clue came to me in the form of a question inscribed on a painting I saw in a pastor's office in Puerto Rico. Just before we went into the sanctuary, my eyes caught a glimpse of it directly in front of his desk. It was the picture of a little girl holding the hand of Jesus, even as He tenderly gazed at her. She was clasping His hand as she asked Him, "*Que paso con tus manos?*"—"What happened to Your hands?"

That question, I suspect, contains the answer to the doubt of the skeptic, the duplicity of the believer, and the despair of the suffering.

It also carries Larry King's question to a more profound level. The virgin birth may only prove to the skeptic that naturalism cannot explain the world's existence and that God has supernaturally intervened in history. In a supernatural framework that is possible. But "What happened to your hands?" answers what it takes to rescue this life of mine from self-serving intellect or from self-glorifying moralizing. It offers a visual answer as to the lengths Christ has gone to reach my own pain, and it brings me to a place from which I no longer live, but Christ lives in me. It buries the self that seeks the self and brings to birth the fullest person that God has so uniquely endowed.

That is to say, in the cross I find my definitive loss that I might obtain my greatest gain. Only when the skeptic and the believer can see those marks that prompt "What happened to your hands?" can life's questions cease and answers pour forth from the depths of the soul.

From talk show hosts to all of us who wrestle with life's questions, the answer is the same. The longer I have lived the more I have come to believe that it is not evidence of which we are short, or the knowledge of discipleship of which we are deprived. For most, what we lack is the courage and peace to go to the cross and to die to ourselves, prompting the world to ask, "What happened to your hands?" There the purpose of history and the purpose of life converge. Our questions will always remain. But these two for me are reminders of where the answers ultimately have to lead.

With this in mind, Calvin Miller said:

The sermon and the Spirit always work in combination to pronounce liberation. Sometimes the Spirit and sermon do supply
direct answers to human need, but most often they answer indi-
rectly. Most problems are not solved by listening to sermons. The
sermon, no matter how sincere, cannot solve these unsolvable
problems. So if the sermon is not a problem solver, where shall
we go for solutions? Together with the Spirit, the sermon exists
to point out that having answers is not essential to living. What is
essential is the sense of God's presence during dark seasons of questioning. . . . Our need for specific answers is dissolved in the greater
issue of the lordship of Christ over all questions—those that have
answers and those that don't.[1]

To Miller's statement I would just change the last line to read,
"Those that have only intellectual answers and those that transcend
the intellect." Or better still, "Those that Bethlehem can answer and
those that only Calvary can."

REFLECTION QUESTIONS

1. Why are Jesus' nail-scarred hands life-defining?
2. What does author Calvin Miller suggest is essential to living? Do you agree?

PERSONAL APPLICATION

1. If you could interview Jesus Christ, what one question would you ask Him?
2. As you wrestle with life's questions or help another work through his or hers, do you believe there is a lack of evidence or perhaps courage to follow through where the answer leads? How might you probe deeper and surrender to God's guidance?

16

JUDGING THE JUDGES

The LORD reigns forever;
he has established his throne for judgment.
He rules the world in righteousness
and judges the peoples with equity.
The LORD is a refuge for the oppressed,
a stronghold in times of trouble.
Those who know your name trust in you,
for you, LORD, have never forsaken those who seek you.

PSALM 9:7-10

During the 2002 Winter Olympics, a major publication featured a headline that read, "Crybaby Olympics." The article highlighted the refrain of complaints launched by several competitors who felt they had been robbed of their legitimate attainment by some unscrupulous judge. In any competition there is always the possibility that someone has been cheated out of winning. Anyone who has ever competed knows the feeling of suspicion when medals are awarded on an inexact basis of measurement. Judging is a hazardous task, but so is judging the judges.

The truth is that judgment calls are part and parcel of most sports. In baseball it's the balls and strikes. The old adage holds true of the umpire who said, "There are balls and there are strikes, and they ain't nothing till I call them." Cricket has that element too. It's too complicated a game to explain in a few words. But anyone who goes to bat knows he can be the victim of a bad call. The hesitancy to leave the batman's box or the home plate speaks volumes that the one called "out" has not taken kindly to the decision. In Toronto when I used to watch hockey, oftentimes when the home crowd disagreed with the referee's call, the organist played "Three Blind Mice," referring to the referee and his two able or "questionable" linesmen.

However legitimate one's complaint might be, the fearful thing is that the winners of the award never seem to stop by the judge's desk and say, "Excuse me, but I really do not think I deserved that." Winners seldom question the validity of the judge's decision. Losers often do.

All this displeasure proves two things. One, we expect a judge to be objective and fair. Two, there is a more serious concern: How does a judge actually judge if there are no absolutes by which to do the judging? You see, it is one thing to measure how far an object has been thrown and another thing to say which was a more beautiful performance on the ice. The latter demands an aesthetic measure, which is not always exact and can be quite subjective.

But you see, deep inside all of us are both of these moral realities. We affirm the need to be right and fair, and we somehow believe that even in beauty there are some misjudgments that reveal prejudice. What this tells us is that life must have absolutes. Even the aesthetic has to find some point of reference.

Interestingly, God in His Word tells us to worship Him in "the beauty of holiness" (Psalm 96:9 KJV). Even beauty has an element of judgment. This itself reveals the fact that we are born as moral agents and when that moral agency is violated—whether in the objective or subjective—deep inside we cry foul.

Judgment is unjust if the judge is corrupt. After all, is that not also the supposed weight of the question "How can God do such a thing?" The writers of the Bible spoke with that quest for justice. "Let me plead my cause," they cry. Job questioned God as thoroughly as anyone, and he was considered one of the most upright ever to have lived.

The Bible makes it clear that God is a Judge and He is fair. One of the most telling passages is in the book of Genesis when God was judging the cities of Sodom and Gomorrah. Abraham was troubled and asked God if He was going to wipe out both the righteous and the unrighteous. God assured Abraham that He saw everything, and Abraham replied, "Will not the Judge of all the earth do right?" (Genesis 18:25). That is the comfort we all need and the moral assurance we may all have. God sees all, knows all, and His judgments are right. It's a word of comfort we must have when we come before Him. May I remind us that reason alone does not work here.

My father-in-law said he had an older brother who was brilliant in any work he assigned. If a heavy toy or game was brought downstairs with which to play, at the end of the enjoyment, he would say, "I brought it down, now you take it up." That worked well until the younger one brought it down. Then the older brother would say, "You brought it down, so it's your responsibility to take it up." No matter what, it always ended up with the younger one having to take it up. Such is the shifting sand of logic when we apply it to others. In more serious matters, the humor vanishes, and the pain emerges.

You and I may not have been robbed of a medal in the Olympics. But we do know that when destiny-defining decisions are made, the Judge of all the earth will do right. We can rest in the knowledge that our Lord is both just and gracious. He knows the absolutes, and He will not make a mistake. That is both comforting and daunting. We must take responsibility, and we must not live in fear or torment when we know the Advocate we have with the Father.

REFLECTION QUESTIONS

1. What does Psalm 9 communicate about God as Judge?
2. Why must there be an absolute standard to rightly judge? How does this standard point to the reality of God's existence?

PERSONAL APPLICATION

1. Consider when you endured unfair judgment, whether in a simple game or a more serious situation. What emotions did you experience? If you still have unresolved anger and mistrust, invite God to bring justice, peace, and healing.
2. Have you wrongly judged someone? How might you make amends and ask forgiveness today?

17

JUSTICE AND VIRTUE

Clearly no one who relies on the law is justified
before God, because "the righteous will
live by faith." The law is not based on faith;
on the contrary, it says, "The person who
does these things will live by them." Christ
redeemed us from the curse of the law by
becoming a curse for us, for it is written:
"Cursed is everyone who is hung on a pole."
He redeemed us in order that the blessing
given to Abraham might come to the Gentiles
through Christ Jesus, so that by faith we
might receive the promise of the Spirit.

GALATIANS 3:11-14

As I mentioned in the previous reading, when poor judging denies an athlete a rightful victory, fans readily sympathize with their hurt. I wish to take it further, into the very heart of all reality. After all the effort and the pain that goes into preparing for competition, it is no doubt a disheartening sight to find dishonesty robbing the reward.

Although such a loss is merely that in athletic competition, it points to the greater need of how important being just really is. This truth is one of the most pertinent in any civilized society. George Washington said, "The due administration of justice is the firmest pillar of good government."[1] Previously, Aristotle had gone even further. He said: "Justice in this sense, then, is not part of virtue but virtue entire, nor is the contrary injustice a part of vice but vice entire."[2]

One does not have to fully agree to note the power of what is being said. Justice is virtue entire? Being just is the sum and substance of good morality? Well, think about this. Suppose you say you love somebody, but you are unjust in your dealings with him or her. How would that person respond to your words, "But I love you"? Or what if you tell somebody that you will always speak the truth, but there will be times you are unjust in dealing with the truth? You see the point, don't you? Justice is an intrinsic part of virtue. You can judge without loving, but you can't love without also being just. That is a painful truth to stomach.

God in His nature is pure and just. His justice meets the demands of the law that must be met, if you and I are to be recipients of His mercy.

To the Christian, Good Friday is a very special day, because on that day two thousand years ago, a pure and just God paid the penalty for our separation from Him and made the way to be forgiven and live in a loving relationship with Him.

There is one verse in the Bible that occurs three times: once in the book of Hebrews to the Hebrew church, once in the book of Galatians to the church in Asia Minor, and once in the book of Romans to the European church. Each time it is a thought quoted from the Old Testament prophet Habakkuk. The verse says simply: "The just shall live by his faith" (2:4 NKJV). That verse comes within the context of Habakkuk asking God how He could witness rampant violence and tolerate wrong and evil. That question troubled Habakkuk, and it is within that context that God said to him that "the vision is yet for an appointed time" (2:3 NKJV).

That is an amazing word of how justice will not ultimately be thwarted. Henry Wadsworth Longfellow once said, "The mills of God grind slowly, yet they grind exceeding small."[3] Elsewhere, the Scriptures remind us: "Whoever remains stiff-necked after many rebukes will suddenly be destroyed—without remedy" (Proverbs 29:1). That is a sobering reminder that God's patience as well has its limit, if justice is to be fulfilled.

That is why the cross is the centerpiece of the gospel message. It is truly the intersection of love and justice, judgment and grace, exactitude and mercy. The demands of the law call for perfection. But the law itself cannot transform the human heart. What this really means is that perfection cannot get us into heaven, but our faith in the Perfect One can. His justice comes hand in hand with love. And neither ever violates the other.

Justice and love came in our Savior. We receive those twin gifts and must dispense them as well. In an amazing way, even the most popular of all verses, John 3:16, has underlying it a legal reality. How beautiful of our Lord to take the strength of the law and give it the Savior's touch. Truly, sublimity at its best.

REFLECTION QUESTIONS

1. You can judge without loving, but you can't love without also being just. Explain.
2. How is the cross the centerpiece of the gospel message?

PERSONAL APPLICATION

1. What are the "twin gifts" Christ offers you? How might you dispense them to others this week?
2. God has a "new day" for you today because Scripture promises His mercies are "new every morning" (Lamentations 3:23). Spend time meditating on Lamentations 3:22–23, and thank God for His mercy and love.

18

BEYOND MORALITY

"Whoever does not take up their cross and
follow me is not worthy of me. Whoever
finds their life will lose it, and whoever
loses their life for my sake will find it."

MATTHEW 10:38-39

As human beings, we have the capacity to feel with moral implications, to exercise the gift of imagination, and to think in paradigms. We make judgments according to the way we each individually view or interpret the world around us. Even if we do not agree with each other on what ought to be, we recognize that there must be—and that there is—an *ought*. For example, we all ought to behave in certain ways or else we cannot get along, which is why we have laws. In short, we ascribe to ourselves freedom with boundaries.

Yet too often we shun boundaries because we feel impeded or we're afraid they will deprive us of what we think we really want. While we know that freedom cannot be absolute, we still resist any notion of limitation—at least for ourselves.

The Bible does not mute its warning here. We are drawn like moths to the flame toward that which often crosses known boundaries, that can destroy, and yet we flirt with those dangers. But at the end of life, we seldom hear regrets for not going into forbidden terrain. I do not know of any Christian at death's threshold who exercised self-control yet wished he or she had been an atheist or had lived an indulgent life. But I have known many in the reverse situation.

In this inconsistency we witness unintended consequences. As I have noted before, I have little doubt that the single greatest obstacle to the impact of the gospel has not been its inability to provide answers, but the failure on our part to live it out. That failure not only robs us of our inner peace but mars the intended light that a consistently lived life brings to the one observing our message.

After lecturing at a major American university, I was driven to the airport by the organizer of the event. I was quite jolted by what he told me. He said, "My wife brought our neighbor last night. She is a medical doctor and had not been to anything like this before. On their way home, my wife asked her what she thought of it all." He paused and then continued, "Do you know what she said?"

Rather reluctantly, I shook my head.

"She said, 'That was a very powerful evening. The arguments were very persuasive. I wonder what he is like in his private life.'"

The answers were intellectually and existentially satisfying, but she still needed to know, did they really make a difference in the life of the one proclaiming them? In other words, the message is seen before it is heard. For any skeptic, the answers to questions are not enough; he or she looks deeper, to the visible transformation of the one offering them.

Here we must bring a different caution. Christianity is definitively and drastically different from all other religions. In every religion except Christianity, morality is a means of attainment. No amount of goodness can justify us before a sovereign God. The Christian message is a reminder that our true malady is one that morality alone cannot solve. Our fundamental problem is not moral; rather, our fundamental problem is spiritual. It is not just that we are immoral, but that a moral life alone cannot bridge what separates us from God. Herein lies the cardinal difference between the moralizing religions and Jesus' offer to us: Jesus does not offer to make bad people good but to make dead people alive.

A heart transformed by God's grace is the efficacious power that lifts us beyond mere morality. It is the richness of being right with God. His grace makes up for what our wills cannot accomplish.

At its core, the call of Jesus is a bountiful invitation to trust and to live in the freedom and riches of that relationship. I am only free inasmuch as I can surrender to God and trust Him to give me the purpose for which my soul longs. This is the wonder and power of a redeemed heart. If I cannot surrender and trust Him, I am not free. We must know to whom we belong and who calls us all to the same purpose. Only when I am at peace with God can I be at peace with myself, and only then will I be at peace with my fellow humans and truly free.

In surrendering to Christ we have the victory over sin. When we die to ourselves, Christ then lives within us. When that crucified life is seen, men and women are drawn to the Savior because they see what the gospel does in a surrendered heart. That witness lives within the boundaries our Lord set for us and takes us beyond mere morality to the life of the soul that is set free.

REFLECTION QUESTIONS

1. What is the single greatest obstacle to the gospel, and what challenge does it present?
2. Why can't morality alone solve our true malady?

PERSONAL APPLICATION

1. The call of Jesus is a bountiful invitation to trust and to live in the freedom of His love. How might you live in light of this truth today?
2. What is it about a surrendered heart that draws people to Christ? Have you experienced this?

19

WHO OWNS YOUR HEART?

Let love and faithfulness never leave you;
bind them around your neck,
write them on the tablet of your heart.
Then you will win favor and a good name
in the sight of God and man.
Trust in the Lord with all your heart
and lean not on your own understanding;
in all your ways submit to him,
and he will make your paths straight.

PROVERBS 3:3-6

In Daniel Goleman's excellent book *Emotional Intelligence*, he writes about Gary and Mary Jean Chauncey, who battled the swirling waters of the river into which the Amtrak train they were on had plummeted. With every bit of energy they had, both fought desperately to save the life of their young daughter Andrea, who had cerebral palsy and was bound to a wheelchair. Somehow they managed to push her out into the arms of rescuers, but sadly, they themselves drowned.

Some would like to explain such heroism as evolution's imprint— we humans behave this way by virtue of evolutionary design for the survival of our progeny. One is hard-pressed not to ask, *Why did the healthier preserve the weaker and not themselves?* But even the author was unable to explain it all in mere Darwinian terms. He added that "only a potent love"[1] could explain such an act.

Indeed, describing this noble act, Goleman points out that such emotionally charged moments do not give birth to impulse in a vacuum, but rather it is the outworking of a commitment to certain values and truths already made in one's life. I believe Goleman is right in this sense. What is most obvious in the love and commitment of these parents to their young one is that passionate commitments never stand alone; they stand on the foundation of a worldview.

In another story, you may recall the chess victory of the computer "Deep Blue" over the world champion Gary Kasparov, which caused many to compare the similarities of machines and humans. Yale professor David Gelernter disagreed. He explained: "The idea that Deep Blue has a mind is absurd. How can an object that wants nothing, fears nothing, enjoys nothing, needs nothing, and cares about nothing have a mind? It can win at chess, but not because it wants to. It isn't happy when it wins or sad when it loses. What are its [post]-match plans if it beats Kasparov? Is it hoping to take Deep Pink out for a night on the town?"[2]

Gelernter continues: "The gap between the human and the surrogate is permanent and will never be closed. Machines will continue to make life easier, healthier, richer, and more puzzling. And humans will continue to care, ultimately, about the same things they always have: about themselves, about one another, and many of them, about God."[3]

Is this not a unique capacity God has put within us—the capacity to feel and to know others intimately? From the selfless sacrifice of loving parents to our own personal thought lives, we recognize that this ability is one aspect of the insurmountable differences between humans and machines—and between the Christian worldview and naturalism.

In the words of the psalmist David, we have been made "a little lower than the angels" (Psalm 8:5). Life, feeling, and thought are God's gifts to us. And where we follow God's thoughts, we feel and act in the highest measure. Moreover, our commitment to God is first and foremost a thing of the heart.

Scripture beckons us: "Trust in the LORD with all your heart and lean not on your own understanding." Nobody understood this better than the man who wrote those words, Solomon. If you look at the book of Proverbs, you'll find the word "heart" again and again. Solomon talked about the heart because he lost his heart to many women. But he urges us, "My son, give me your heart" (Proverbs 23:26). This is because our entire spiritual journey and the threads that God wants to pull together will be determined by who owns our hearts.

My question to you today is, *Who owns your heart?* To whom does your heart belong? How will you know the answer to the question? It is what Solomon said: "In all your ways submit to him." It is the path you choose, the decisions you make, the way you live. If you do not acknowledge God, your heart belongs to something or someone other than to Him.

REFLECTION QUESTIONS

1. In what way is the Christian worldview different from naturalism?
2. Why are our hearts' commitments so life-defining?

PERSONAL APPLICATION

1. Consider memorizing Proverbs 3:3–6 or placing these words where you can see them often.
2. How would you answer the question "Who owns your heart?" Allow this question to direct your steps today.

20

DISPARATE THREADS

"Because I live, you also will live."

JOHN 14:19

Some years ago, I was visiting a place known for making the best wedding saris in the world. They were the producers of saris rich in gold and silver threads, resplendent with an array of colors. With such intricacy of product, I expected to see some elaborate system of machines that would boggle the mind in production. But this image could not have been further from the real scene.

Each sari was made individually by a father-and-son team. The father sat above the son on a platform, surrounded by several spools of thread that he would gather into his fingers. The son had only one task. At a nod from his father, he would move the shuttle from one side to the other and back again. This would then be repeated for hundreds of hours, until a magnificent pattern began to emerge.

The son certainly had the easier task. He was only to move at the father's nod. But making use of these efforts, the father was working to an artful end. All along, he had the design in his mind and was bringing the right threads together.

The more I reflect on my own life and study the lives of others, I am fascinated to see the design God has for each one of us individually, if we would only respond. All through our days, little reminders show the threads that God has woven into our lives.

Allow me to share a story from my own experience. As one searching for meaning in the throes of a turbulent adolescence, I found myself on a hospital bed from an attempted suicide. It was there that I was read John 14:19, and my attention was fully captured by what Jesus said to His disciples: "Because I live, ye shall live also." I turned my life over to Christ that day, committing my pains, struggles, and pursuits to His able hands.

Almost thirty years to the day after this decision, my wife and I were in India and decided to visit my grandmother's grave. With the help of a gardener we walked through the accumulated weeds and rubble until we found the stone marking her grave. With his bucket of water and a small brush, the gardener cleared off the years of caked-on dirt. To our utter surprise, under her name, a verse gradually appeared. My wife clasped my hand and said, "Look at the verse!" It read: "Because I live, ye shall live also."

If an ordinary weaver can create out of a collection of colored threads a garment that will beautify the face, can the Grand Weaver not have a design in mind for you, a design that will adorn you, as He uses your life to fashion you, using all the threads He has within His reach? A purposeful design emerges when the Father weaves a pattern from what to us may often seem disparate threads.

REFLECTION QUESTIONS

1. What does the father alone see in his work as a weaver?
2. What did Jesus mean when He told His disciples, "Because I live, you also will live"?

PERSONAL APPLICATION

1. What has the Grand Weaver done in your life to reveal His handiwork and design?
2. We are reminded that God is at work in places of beauty as well as pain. Who needs God's touch today, and how might you reach out?

21

THE HUNGERING SPIRIT

Jesus declared, "I am the bread of
life. Whoever comes to me will never
go hungry, and whoever believes
in me will never be thirsty."

I have pondered long and hard the question of why people turn to God. I remember a woman from Romania telling me that she was raised in a staunchly atheistic environment. The family members were not allowed to even mention the name of God in their household, lest they be overheard and their entire education denied. After she came to the United States, I happened to be her patient when I was recovering from back surgery. When I had the privilege of praying with her one day, she said as she wiped away her tears, "Deep in my heart I have always believed there was a God. I just didn't know how to find Him."

This sentiment is repeated scores of times. I had the great privilege of meeting with two very key people in an avowedly atheistic country. After I finished praying, one of them said, "I have never prayed in my entire life, and I have never heard anyone else pray. This is a first for me. Thank you for teaching me how to pray." It was obvious that even spiritual hungers that have been suppressed for an entire lifetime are in evidence in a situation where there is possible fulfillment.

Although I agree that the problem of pain may be one of the greatest challenges to faith in God, I dare suggest that it is the problem of pleasure that more often drives us to think of spiritual things. Sexuality, greed, fame, and momentary thrills are actually the most precarious attractions in the world. Pain forces us to accept our finitude. It can breed cynicism, weariness, and fatigue in just living. Pain sends us in search of a greater power. Introspection, superstition, ceremony, and vows can all come as a result of pain.

But disappointment in pleasure is a completely different thing. While pain can often be seen as a means to a greater end, pleasure is seen as an end in itself. And when pleasure has run its course, a sense of despondency can creep into one's soul that may often lead to self-destruction. Pain can often be temporary, but disappointment in pleasure gives rise to emptiness—not just for a moment, but for life. There can seem to be no reason to life, no preconfigured purpose, if even pleasure brings no lasting fulfillment.

The intertwining of pain with pleasure is at the root of the human dilemma and at the core of the hungering spirit. People in pain may look for comfort and explanations. People disappointed in pleasure look for purpose. In our boredom, we may search for an escape in the strange or the distorted, while God has revealed Himself in the person of Jesus Christ.

Only in the Judeo-Christian worldview is every person understood to be created in God's image, for God Himself is a person. Likewise, each person has *relational* priorities that are implicitly built in, not by nature but by God's design. Consider the tragedy of the earthquake and tsunami in Japan some years ago. Even in that stoic culture, where community rises above everything else, each one who wept was grieving the loss of loved ones: they were not grieving just for the total loss of life but also for their personal loss. This is real. It is not imaginary. We stand before the individual graves of the ones we love more often than we stand before a graveyard in general.

But there is more. Personhood transcends mere DNA. There is essential *worth* to each person. In Christianity, the essence of each and every person, the individual reality of each life, is sacred. It is sacred because intrinsic value has been given to us by our Creator, who has revealed Himself in the starry skies and upon a nail-scarred cross.

The more I reflect on my own life and interact with others, I am fascinated to see the design God has for each one of us individually, if we would only respond. The truth is that I have known people who in the peak of their success have turned to God, and I have known others, drowning in pain and defeat, who seek God for an answer. Either extreme leaves haunting questions. God alone knows how we will respond to either.

God has created us for His purpose, and relationship and worship are built into this design. God alone can weave a pattern from the diverse strands of our lives—whether suffering, success, joy, or heartache—and fashion a magnificent design. Perhaps today, if you will stop and reflect on it, you will see that He is seeking your hungering spirit.

REFLECTION QUESTIONS

1. What does it mean to be made in God's image, and what does the Christian worldview uniquely say about personhood?
2. For what purpose did God create us? How does praying for people open their hearts to God's purpose for them?

PERSONAL APPLICATION

1. The problem of pain and the problem of pleasure both present distinct challenges to surrendering our hearts to God. What obstacles have you experienced or witnessed in others? Are these still obstacles to trusting God's love and grace?
2. Have you prayed with someone who wouldn't identify as a Christian and seen a similar response? Pray for an opportunity to reach out with God's love in this way.

22

THE MOST DIFFICULT QUESTIONS

Now we see only a reflection as in a mirror;
then we shall see face to face. Now I know in
part; then I shall know fully, even as I am fully
known. And now these three remain: faith,
hope and love. But the greatest of these is love.

1 CORINTHIANS 13:12-13

Out of the scores of letters I have received over the years, one in particular stands out. The writer simply asked why God made it so difficult to believe in Him. He noted that if he loved somebody and had infinite power, he would use that power to show himself more obviously. He wondered, *Why has God made it so difficult to see His presence and His plan?*

It is a powerful question that is both felt and intellectual at the same time. One might say, "Why is God so hidden?" The question ultimately gains momentum and parks itself in our hearts' genuine search for meaning, belonging, and relationship to our own Creator.

I recall the restlessness and turning point of my own life. I had come to believe that life had no meaning. Nothing seemed to connect. As you've read, when still in my teens I found myself lying in a hospital bed after an attempted suicide. The struggle for answers when met by despair led me along that tragic path. But there in my hospital room the Scriptures were brought and read to me. For the first time I engaged the direct answers of God to my seeking heart. The profound realization of the news that God could be known personally drew me, with sincerity and determination, to plumb the depths of that claim. With a simple prayer of trust, in that moment, the change from a desperate heart to one that found the fullness of meaning became a reality for me.

The immediate change was in the new way I saw God's handiwork. The marvel of discovering even splendor in the ordinary was the work of God in my heart. Over a period of time, I was able to study, pursue, and understand how to respond to more intricate questions of the mind.

That divine encounter of coming to know Him brought meaning and made answers reachable. I believe God intervenes in each of our lives. He speaks to us in different ways and at different times so that we may know that He is the Author of our very personalities; that His answers are both propositional and relational (and sometimes in reverse order); that His presence stills the storms of the heart.

Oddly enough, in history the most questioning and the resistant became God's mouthpieces to skeptics. Consider Peter, Paul, and Thomas—just to name a few. They questioned, they wrestled, they challenged. But once convinced, they spoke and wrote and persuaded people in the most difficult of circumstances. That is why they willingly paid the ultimate price, even as they sought God's power and presence in those "dark nights of the soul."[1]

In the end, in the face of difficult questions, the answers that are given and received must be both felt and real, with the firm knowledge that God is nearer than one might think. Yes, the Scriptures reveal, as many can attest, that this assurance of His nearness sometimes comes at a cost, as in any relationship of love and commitment. But God desires that we know Him and that He is not distant from us. He is grander than any wondrous sight we may behold and the answer to every heart's deepest question.

The final consummation of that glimpse is yet future. I firmly believe as the apostle Paul declared: "Eye has not seen and ear has not heard, and which have not entered the heart of man, all that God has prepared for those who love Him" (1 Corinthians 2:9 NASB). Then we shall see, not darkly, but face-to-face. That is when the soul will feel the ultimate touch, and the silence will be one of knowing with awesome wonder. The only thing we would want hidden is how blind we were.

REFLECTION QUESTIONS

1. God has revealed Himself through His Word, through Jesus Christ, His Spirit in the life of the church, and even His created world. Is God hidden?
2. What does it mean to say that God's answers are both propositional and relational?

PERSONAL APPLICATION

1. If God seems hidden from you personally, is there someone who can pray for you? How might you rest in God's presence today? (Consider reading Psalms 23 and 139.)
2. Spend time reflecting on the truth that God is the answer to your heart's deepest question. Where or to whom might you turn to seek answers to your questions?

23

THE THROES OF WONDER

How many are your works, Lord!
In wisdom you made them all;
the earth is full of your creatures.
There is the sea, vast and spacious,
teeming with creatures beyond number—
living things both large and small. . . .
May the glory of the Lord endure forever;
may the Lord rejoice in his works—
he who looks at the earth, and it trembles,
who touches the mountains, and they smoke.

PSALM 104:24-25, 31-32

have had the privilege of crisscrossing this globe over four decades and seeing much of the world. I have frequently been asked about my favorite city or what food I enjoy the most. The latter is easier to answer than the former because, while cities have attractions for different reasons, the palate is often influenced by one's land of birth.

Strangely, I have never been asked about my favorite site. I am not sure I could pick a single spectacle, but I know one experience that would be in the running as the most emotionally moving moment for me. On a brilliantly sunny day, my colleague and I were driven from Cape Town to very near land's end in South Africa: Cape Point. There we stood at the edge of terra firma and watched as the waters of the calmer Atlantic and the restless Indian Ocean collided into one massive torrent of fluid strength, the power of the current almost visible to the naked eye. That body of water has been the graveyard of many mariners trying to navigate their way around the globe. The endless horizon, the borderless blue and turquoise of the mighty waters, and the frothy white tips of the crashing waves as they collided against each other—this scene from the world's end seemed just to overwhelm us with a stupendous sense of awe.

Yes, I have seen the Taj Mahal and many of the other so-called wonders of the world. But this was sheer enchantment, not made by human hand! Whether it was because we were not expecting such a banquet for the eyes, or whether it was that we needed refreshment after a busy day, I would not even venture to analyze. All I know is that it affected both of us in the same way.

For seemingly unexplainable reasons, my eyes filled with tears. I was in the throes of enjoying the wonder and the vastness of creation. I felt at once both dwarfed and elevated—dwarfed because my entire stature as a human being seemed so diminished compared to this display of beauty and power before me, but elevated because I could revel in this glorious sight—while the land and water combined could not exult in their own beauty or share in any delight.

But then a strange, unexpected sensation took hold of us, and we both did something that neither of us had ever done before. We walked back a few steps, found a sharp stone, and scratched the names of our wives onto the surface of a massive piece of rock. We realized that in a matter of days the writing would be erased, but the thought and act spoke volumes. We had been in the throes of wonder and it just seemed incomplete that we could not enjoy it with the ones dearest to us and express something from the overflow.

Questions of personal choice—"What is your favorite destination?"—are relatively easy to answer. After all, one is answering from his or her own context and delights. But then there emerge questions such as "How can I know God exists?" or "Why is there evil in this world?" The answers call for some universal implication. Such questions are indicative of the struggles of many skeptics as well as believers and reveal that the deepest questions can span both the mind and the heart.

Questioning is the way of humanity. We will always ask, debate, challenge, and search. And yet there is an immense difference between a worldview that is not able to answer every question to complete satisfaction and one with answers that are consistently contradictory. There is an even greater difference between answers that contain paradoxes and those that are systemically irreconcilable.

Once again, the Christian faith stands out as unique in this test, both as a system of thought and in the answers it provides. Christianity does not promise that you will have every question fully answered to your satisfaction before you die, but the answers it gives are consistently consistent. There may be paradoxes within Christian teaching and belief, but they are not irreconcilable.

I often put it this way: God has put enough into this world to make faith in Him a most reasonable thing. But He has left enough out to make it impossible to live by sheer reason alone. Faith and reason must always work together in that plausible blend.

Deep within every human heart throbs the undying hope that somebody or something will bring both an explanation of what life is all about and a way to retain the wonder. Yet if we would but pause and first ponder what we already see in this world of wonder, we might get a brief taste of the wonder that may be poured into us as well.

The connecting of faith and reason is the wonderful journey of the soul. When one's thinking is set aright again and when the flesh has its shackles broken, the mind and body come under God's liberating and fulfilling plan. Then we see as He designed us to see. When we come to know our Creator, the questioning is not for doubting but for putting it all together and marveling at His wonders.

REFLECTION QUESTIONS

1. What do you think compels us to etch the names of those we love in stone? How does this impulse relate to the act of worship and being made in God's image?
2. Contrary to what the naturalist or atheist may say, why is it impossible to live by sheer reason alone?

PERSONAL APPLICATION

1. Is there a destination or familiar place that inspires you to worship? What is it about this setting that draws you toward God?
2. Read Psalm 104 and ask God to open your eyes to the majesty of His creation and providential care.

24

FROM PROXIMATE
TO PERSONAL

Jesus answered, "Everyone who drinks this
water will be thirsty again, but whoever drinks
the water I give them will never thirst. Indeed,
the water I give them will become in them a
spring of water welling up to eternal life."
The woman said to him, "Sir, give me this water
so that I won't get thirsty and have to keep
coming here to draw water."

JOHN 4:13-15

Some time ago my wife, Margie, returned from an errand visibly shaken by a heartrending conversation she had experienced. She was about the very simple task of selecting a picture and a frame when a dialogue began with the owner of the shop. When Margie said she would like a scene with children in it, the woman quite casually asked if the people for whom the picture was being purchased had any children of their own. "No," replied my wife, "but that is not by their choice."

There was a momentary pause. Suddenly, like a hydrant uncorked, a question burst with unveiled hostility from the woman's lips: "Have you ever lost a child?"

Margie was somewhat taken aback and immediately sensed that a terrible tragedy lurked behind the abrupt question.

The conversation had obviously taken an unsettling turn. But even at that my wife was not prepared for the flood of emotion and anger that was to follow, from this one who was still a stranger. The sorry tale quickly unfolded. The woman proceeded to speak of the two children she had lost, each loss carrying a heartache all its own. "Now," she added, "I am watching my sister as she is about to lose her child." There was no masking of her bitterness and no hesitancy about where she ascribed the blame for these tragedies.

Unable to utter anything that would alleviate the pain of this gaping wound in the woman's heart, my wife began to say, "I am sorry" when she was interrupted with a stern rebuke, "Don't say anything!" She finally managed to say in parting, "I'll be praying for you through this difficult time." But even that brought a crisp rejoinder: "Don't bother."

Margie returned to her car and wept out of shock and longing to reach out to this broken life. Even more, ever since that conversation she has carried with her an unshakable mental picture of a woman's face in which every muscle contorted with anger and anguish—at once seeking a touch yet holding back, yearning for consolation but silencing anyone who sought to help, shoving at people along the way to get to God.

Strangely, this episode spawned a friendship, and we have had the wonderful privilege of getting close to this woman and praying with her in our home. We have even felt her embrace of gratitude as she has tried in numerous ways to say, "Thank you." But through this all she has represented to us a symbol of smothered cries and of a search for answers that need time before anger is overcome by trust and anguish gives way to contentment.

Likewise, as I have often said, every face is a reminder that behind every question, whether veiled or direct, is a questioner—and one must always seek to respond to the individual and not merely the question.

Of all the stories in the Scriptures, none so reflects those varied needs of humanity as the story of the woman at the well in her conversation with Jesus. In the fourth chapter of John's gospel, we read of the encounter Jesus had with the Samaritan woman. The disciples had left Him while they went into town to buy food. When they returned they were astounded to see Him talking to this Samaritan woman, but they were afraid to ask why He would talk to her or to question what prompted this curious familiarity.

The woman represented all that was oppressed or rejected in that society. She was a woman, not a man. She was a Samaritan burdened with ethnic rejection. She was discarded and broken from five different marriages. She identified God with a particular location, not having the faintest clue how to reach this God. Was it possible to have any less self-esteem in her fragmented world?

Jesus began His tender yet determined task to dislodge her from the well-doctored and cosmetically dressed-up theological jargon she threw at Him, so she could voice the real cry of her heart. Almost as if He were peeling off the layers of an onion, He steadily moved her away from her own fears and prejudices, from her own schemes for self-preservation, from her own ploys for hiding her hurts, to the radiant and thrilling source of her greatest fulfillment, Christ Himself. In short, He moved her from the abstract to the concrete, from the concrete to the proximate, from the proximate to the personal. She had come to find water for the thirst of her body. He fulfilled a greater thirst, that of her soul.

In the Psalms, David described himself as one wounded and crying in his bed at night. This same David spoke of the happiness that came when he took his cry to the Lord. With these reminders from Scriptures, let us examine our own hearts. We might be surprised to know how much bottled-up sentiment will be uncovered. When God speaks, we need not respond by saying, "Don't say a thing"; rather, we can rest in God's comfort, knowing that God listens to our cries and comes near in our need.

REFLECTION QUESTIONS

1. Reflect upon "Some answers need time before anger is overcome by trust" and "Behind every question is a questioner."
2. How did Jesus tenderly reveal the Samaritan woman's heart and allow her to see her deepest need?

PERSONAL APPLICATION

1. A wise counselor or trusted friend can help us to see ourselves as we truly are. Do you have unresolved heartache or anger that needs to be brought to light so you can experience your heavenly Father's healing?
2. How might you be a "Margie" this week to someone in need of a listening ear and Christ's compassion and prayer?

A BIGGER STORY

Faith is confidence in what we hope for and assurance about what we do not see. This is what the ancients were commended for. By faith we understand that the universe was formed at God's command, so that what is seen was not made out of what was visible. . . . Without faith it is impossible to please God, because anyone who comes to him must believe that he exists and that he rewards those who earnestly seek him.

HEBREWS 11:1-3, 6

The story is told of a man who was fishing. Every time he caught a big fish, he threw it back into the water. Every little fish he caught went into his bag. Another big one, back into the water; a tiny one, into his bag. Finally, a man who had been watching him and was very perplexed by his unorthodox manner of fishing asked, "Can you please explain to me why you are throwing the big ones away?" The fisherman did not hesitate: "Because I only have an eight-inch frying pan, and anything bigger than eight inches does not fit my pan!"

We may chuckle at someone who throws away a fish too big for a pan or someone else who just explains away anything that doesn't fit his or her own prejudiced opinions. Yet we see this repeatedly: the naturalists who describe the origins of the universe as "unrepeatable" or "almost a miracle" or "mathematically impossible" but will simply fight off any possibility of agency or cause or the supernatural. The question that always demands an answer and that each one of us must pause to ask ourselves is whether our paradigm of the world matches reality. Does it fit? Is there explanatory power for the unshakable questions of life? Is it coherent? Is it rationally livable?

But there is a rub. We must recognize that every worldview can leave us with questions that we cannot exhaustively resolve this side of eternity. Every worldview has gaps. The question is, *Does my paradigm fit reality and have enough reason behind it to explain how these gaps might actually be filled and remain consistent?*

What do I mean by *gaps*? Let me borrow an illustration from Francis Schaeffer. Suppose you were to leave a room with two glasses on the table, Glass A and Glass B. Glass A has two ounces of water in it, and Glass B is empty. When you return at the end of the day, Glass B now has water in it and Glass A is empty. You could assume that someone took the water from Glass A and put it into Glass B. That, however, does not fully explain the situation, because you notice that Glass B now has four ounces of water in it, whereas Glass A had only two ounces in it when you left in the morning.

You are confronted with a problem that at best has only a partial explanation. Whether the water from Glass A was poured into Glass B is debatable. But what is beyond debate is that all of the water in Glass B could not have come from Glass A. The additional two ounces had to have come from elsewhere.

The Christian worldview presents a powerful and unique explanation of these other "two ounces." Naturalism may be able to explain the two ounces in Glass B. It cannot explain the four ounces in it. The theistic framework is not only credible but also far more adept than atheism or other worldviews in dealing with the real questions of life: questions of origin, meaning, morality, and destiny. Whichever starting point we take—either the philosophical followed by the biblical or the biblical by itself, which for many is sufficient—the cogency and convincing power of the answers emerge very persuasively. The original "two ounces," as well as the additional "two ounces," are best explained in a Christian theistic framework. The arguments range from the simple to the intricate, depending on the question and its context.

I will repeat what I've said before: God has put enough into the world to make faith in Him a most reasonable thing. But He has left enough out to make it impossible to live by sheer reason or observation alone. You will recall, for example, that the resurrection of Jesus caught even the disciples by surprise. They did not believe at first that Jesus had risen from the dead. Their understanding of reality was foundationally challenged. All of life and destiny would now have to be reinterpreted. They thought that perhaps Jesus' resurrection was some fanciful story conjured up by hallucinating people. Their entire hope in Him was politically based—that Jesus would somehow overthrow Rome. But a political victory would have been only a superficial solution, for Jesus came to open the eyes of the blind and to transform hearts and minds. I wonder whether multiple evidences that Jesus had risen from the dead would make any difference to modern-day atheists, or would they be tossed away because of an "eight inch" measuring container?

You see, the problem with evidence is that it is very much limited to the moment and creates the demand for repeated intervention of some sort. I have seen this in my own life over and over. Today it may be a failing business that is in need of God's intervention. Tomorrow I may want to be healed from cancer. The day after that, I may even want a loved one to be brought back from the dead. There is an insatiable hunger for the constancy of the miracle.

The gospel is true and beautiful and has enough of the miracle to ground it in sufficient reason. But it is also sometimes a hard road because of the intertwining of reason and faith.

When we come to those places in the road where we long for another "proof," I pray that we might know that rising beyond reason (to be sure, not violating it) is the constancy of trust in God, and we might sense His presence, for that is really the greater miracle within us. Only through exercising that trust can the moment be accepted and understood as a small portion of a bigger story. For some of us, that individual story may entail a long and arduous journey, but it will be accomplished one moment at a time, one day at a time, each moment and day undergirded by the strength of the indwelling presence of God.

Even Peter realized that the delight of the transfiguration had to be transcended by "a more sure word of prophecy" (2 Peter 1:19 KJV). He believed that Word even on the road to martyrdom, confident that his life was part of God's bigger story. This is the hope of gospel: "Faith is confidence in what we hope for and assurance about what we do not see."

REFLECTION QUESTIONS

1. How does the Christian worldview best make sense of the two ounces of water in the illustration?
2. What is faith according to Hebrews 11?

PERSONAL APPLICATION

1. What is the "greater miracle within us," and how might this reality guide you today?
2. Even the disciples' paradigm of Jesus was challenged. Where do you need to grow in the constancy of trust in God?

26

ALL THINGS NEW

We regard no one from a worldly point of view.
Though we once regarded Christ in this way,
we do so no longer. Therefore, if anyone is in
Christ, the new creation has come: The old
has gone, the new is here! All this is from God,
who reconciled us to himself through Christ
and gave us the ministry of reconciliation.

2 CORINTHIANS 5:16–18

s the Christian faith intellectual nonsense? Does God really trans-form us?

Atheist Sam Harris declares, "Everything of value that people get from religion can be had more honestly, without presuming anything on insufficient evidence. The rest is self-deception, set to music."[1]

Richard Dawkins suggests that the idea of God is a virus, and we need to find software to eradicate it. Somehow if we can expunge the virus that led us to think this way, we will be purified and rid of this bedeviling notion of God, good, and evil.[2] Along with a few others, these atheists call for the banishment of all religious belief. "Away with this nonsense" is their battle cry. In return, they promise a world of new hope and unlimited horizons once we have shed this delusion of God.

I have news for them, however—news to the contrary. The reality is that the emptiness that results from the loss of the transcendent is stark and devastating, philosophically and existentially. Indeed, the denial of an objective moral law, based on the compulsion to deny the existence of God, results ultimately in the denial of evil itself. In an attempt to escape what atheists call the contradiction between a good God and a world of evil, they try to dance around the reality of a moral law (and hence, a moral Lawgiver) by introducing terms like "evolutionary ethics." The one who raises the question against God in effect plays God while denying God exists.

Now one may wonder: *Why do you actually need a moral Lawgiver if you have a moral law?* The answer is because the questioner and the issue he questions always involve the essential value of a person. You can never talk of morality in abstraction. Persons are implicit to the question and the object of the question. In a nutshell, positing a moral law without a moral Lawgiver would be equivalent to raising the question of evil without a questioner. So you cannot have a moral law unless the moral law itself is intrinsically woven into personhood, which means it demands an intrinsically worthy person if the moral law itself is valued. And that person can only be God.

In reality, our inability to alter what is actual frustrates our grandiose delusions of being sovereign over everything. Yet the truth is we cannot escape the existential rub by running from a moral law. Objective moral values exist only if God exists. Is it all right, for example, to mutilate babies for entertainment? Every reasonable person will say no. We know that objective moral values do exist. Therefore, God must exist. Examining those premises and their validity presents a very strong argument.

The world does not understand what the absoluteness of the moral law is all about. Some get caught, some don't get caught. Yet who of us would like our hearts exposed on the front page of the newspaper today? Have there not been days and hours when, like the apostle Paul, you've struggled within yourself and said, "I do not understand what I do. For what I want to do I do not do, but what I hate I do. . . . What a wretched man I am! Who will rescue me from this body . . . [of] death?" (Romans 7:15, 24). Each of us knows this tension and conflict within if we are honest with ourselves.

In that spirit, we ought to take time to reflect seriously upon the questions, *Has God truly wrought a miracle in my life? Is my own heart proof of the supernatural intervention of God?* In the West where we go through seasons of newfangled theologies, the whole question of the "lordship" of Christ plagued our debates for some time as we asked, *Is there such a thing as a minimalist view of conversion?* That is, "We said the prayer and that's it." Yet how can there be a minimalist view of conversion when conversion itself is a maximal work of God's grace? Scripture declares that when we come to experience God's saving grace, "Old things are passed away; behold, all things are become new" (2 Corinthians 5:17 KJV). In a strange way we have minimized every sacred commitment and made it the lowest common denominator. *What might my new birth mean to me?* That is a question we seldom ask. *Who was I before God's work in me, and who am I now?*

The first entailment of coming to know the God of transformation is the new hungers and new pursuits that are planted within the human will. I well recall that dramatic change in my own way of thinking. There were new longings, new hopes, new dreams, new fulfillments, but most noticeably a new will to do what was God's will. This new affection of heart—the love of God wrought in us through the Holy Spirit—expels all other old seductions and attractions. Those who know Jesus Christ begin to see that their own misguided hearts are impoverished and in need of constant submission to the will of the Lord—spiritual surrender.

The hallmark of conversion is to see one's own spiritual poverty. Arrogance and conceit ought to be inimical to the life of the believer. A deep awareness of one's own new hungers and longings is a convincing witness both to God and God's grace within.

REFLECTION QUESTIONS

1. Why must the reality of evil be denied if we deny an objective moral law?
2. Why must there be a moral Lawgiver (God) if a moral law exists?

PERSONAL APPLICATION

1. Who was I before God's work in me, and who am I now?
2. How might you be a convincing witness to others this week?

27

DOES PRAYER MATTER?

"Ask and it will be given to you; seek and you
will find; knock and the door will be opened
to you. For everyone who asks receives;
the one who seeks finds; and to the one
who knocks, the door will be opened.
"Which of you fathers, if your son asks for a fish,
will give him a snake instead? Or if he asks for an
egg, will give him a scorpion? If you then, though
you are evil, know how to give good gifts to
your children, how much more will your Father in
heaven give the Holy Spirit to those who ask him!"

LUKE 11:9–13

sat with a man in my car, talking about a series of heartbreaks he had experienced. "There were just a few things I had wanted in life," he said. "None of them have turned out the way I had prayed. I wanted my parents to live until I was at least able to stand on my own and they could watch my children grow up. It didn't happen. I wanted my marriage to succeed, and it didn't. I wanted my children to grow up grateful for what God had given them. That didn't happen. I wanted my business to prosper, and it didn't. Not only have my prayers amounted to nothing; the exact opposite has happened. Don't even ask if you can pray for me. I am left with no trust of any kind in such things."

I felt two emotions rising up within me as I listened. The first was one of genuine sorrow. He felt that he had tried, that he had done his part, but that God hadn't lived up to His end of the deal. The second emotion was one of helplessness, as I wondered where to begin trying to help him.

These are the sharp edges of faith in a transcendent, all-powerful, personal God. Most of us have a tendency to react with anger or withdrawal when we feel God has let us down by not giving us things we felt were legitimate requests. We may feel guilty that our expectations of God were too great. We may feel that God has not answered our prayers because of something lacking in ourselves. We may compare ourselves with others whose every wish seems to be granted by God and wonder why He hasn't come through for us in the same way. And sometimes we allow this disappointment in God to fester and eat away at our faith in Him until the years go by and we find ourselves bereft of belief.

G. K. Chesterton surmised that when belief in God becomes difficult, the tendency is to turn away from Him—but, in heaven's name, to what? To the skeptic or the one who has been disappointed in his faith, the obvious answer may be to give up believing that there's somebody out there, take charge of your own life, and live it out to the best of your own ability.

But Chesterton also wrote, "The real trouble with this world of ours is not that it is an unreasonable world, nor even that it is a reasonable one. The commonest kind of trouble is that it is nearly reasonable, but not quite."[1] He is right. Only so much about life can be understood by reason; so much falls far short of any reasonable explanation.

Prayer then becomes the irrepressible cry of the heart at the times we most need it. Prayer is far more complex than some make it out to be. There is much more involved than merely asking for something and receiving it. In this, as in other contexts, we too often succumb to believing that something is what it never was, even when we know it cannot be as simple as we would like to think it is.

For every person who feels that prayer has not "worked" for him and has therefore abandoned God, there is someone else for whom prayer remains a vital part of her life, sustaining her even when her prayers have gone unanswered, because her belief and trust are not only in the power of prayer but in the character and wisdom of God. When God is the focus of our prayer, I believe He sustains and preserves our faith.

REFLECTION QUESTIONS

1. What does Luke 11 tell us about both prayer and about the character of God?
2. Prayer remains a vital part of our lives when what elements of belief are in focus?

PERSONAL APPLICATION

1. How have you handled disappointment in prayer?
2. Are there areas of your life awaiting God's healing touch? Do you know someone who needs to be encouraged in prayer and reminded of God's goodness?

28

THE SPIRIT OF PRAYER

"Our Father in heaven,
hallowed be your name,
your kingdom come,
your will be done,
on earth as it is in heaven.
Give us today our daily bread.
And forgive us our debts,
as we also have forgiven our debtors.
And lead us not into temptation,
but deliver us from the evil one."

MATTHEW 6:9–13

Early church father John Chrysostom, archbishop of Constantinople in the fourth century, wrote this about the power of prayer:

> Prayer is an all-efficient panoply, a treasure undiminished, a mine which is never exhausted, a sky unobscured by the clouds, a heaven unruffled by the storm. It is the root, the fountain, the mother of a thousand blessings. . . . The potency of prayer hath subdued the strength of fire, it hath bridled the rage of lions, hushed anarchy to rest; extinguished wars, appeased the elements, expelled demons, burst the chains of death, expanded the gates of heaven, assuaged diseases, repelled frauds, rescued cities from destruction, stayed the sun in its course, and arrested the progress of the thunderbolt.[1]

Who can read that and not be tempted to exclaim, *What rhetoric!* No, not so. Each of the instances referred to by Chrysostom is drawn right out of the Scriptures.

In all of its expressions, whether halting and short or flowing in beautiful, well-structured phrases, prayer is simply a conversation with God. If we turn prayer into a monologue, or use it as a way to showcase our gift with words, or as a venue for informing or instructing others who may be listening, we defeat the very purpose of prayer. The Bible makes it clear that prayer is intended as the line of connection from the heart of the praying person directly to the heart of God. Jesus Himself practiced a lifestyle of prayer and urged His disciples to imitate Him by making it part of their daily existence. His prayers represented prayer at its best and most sincere.

I marvel at the impact of praying with a hurting person. I have prayed many times with someone who has claimed to be a skeptic and is living in a manner that supports that claim, only to finish my prayer and open my eyes to see tears in his eyes. Although prayer remains a mystery to all of us but especially to one who lives apart from God, I have observed again and again that even the hardened heart retains a longing for the possibility of communicating with God.

It is not my intention to deny the great disappointments of unanswered prayer, but let us look at what God intends prayer to be. The most definitive passage is what is often called the Lord's Prayer or, as some scholars like to call it, the Disciples' Prayer. The highly significant first words carry the weight of all of prayer: "Our Father in heaven." This is a uniquely Christian utterance. In these two words alone—"Our Father"—we recognize, at least implicitly, two truths: the nearness of God as heavenly Father, and the sovereignty of God as the One who controls everything. As soon as you cry out in prayer, "Heavenly Father," you are recognizing His presence in your life.

After the Lord's Prayer and as His conclusion to it, Jesus told us that God would give the Holy Spirit, His indwelling presence, to those who ask for it (Luke 11:13). It is not spoken in the form of a question—it ends with an exclamation point! God will give the gift of the indwelling presence of the holy God to any who ask for it—this is an absolute certainty! You can count on it!

Sadly, we hear so little of this today. We have turned prayer into a means to our ends and seldom wait on God's response long enough to think about what He wants for us in that very moment. By reducing the evidence of the indwelling of the Holy Spirit to one particular gift, we have robbed people of the Holy Presence that prompts us in prayer, prays for us when we don't have the words to pray for ourselves, and comforts us in our times of need.

The paramount need today is the indwelling presence of God. In this incredible twist, the indwelling presence of God, the Holy Spirit, makes God both the Enabler of our prayers and the Provider of answers to those prayers. More than anything else, this is what prayer is about.

REFLECTION QUESTIONS

1. What does Jesus' teaching on prayer communicate about God? What does it say about our needs?
2. What is the ultimate gift in prayer that God wants to give us (see Luke 11:13)? What does this perspective say about God's desires for His children?

PERSONAL APPLICATION

1. Chrysostom wrote that prayer is a splendid display of God's treasure and power. Have you witnessed this? Take time to read the prophet Daniel's prayers or about John Chrysostom's life and writings.
2. It's easy to turn prayer into a means to an end. How can the reminder of God's indwelling presence change the way you pray today?

29

REARRANGING THE FURNITURE

The Lord looked with favor on Abel and his offering, but on Cain and his offering he did not look with favor. So Cain was very angry, and his face was downcast. Then the Lord said to Cain, ". . . If you do what is right, will you not be accepted? But if you do not do what is right, sin is crouching at your door; it desires to have you, but you must rule over it."

GENESIS 4:4–7

History has a way of provoking life's most basic questions, sometimes with deadly force. Standing beside ruins and devastation, newscasters daily relay horrors. As harsh realities take hold, the irrepressible *Why?* often surfaces. Occasionally, even international conscience is so aroused as to ask, *Why?*

Yet in reality, the question of *Why?* in a violent act, as painful as such a mindless atrocity can be, is nevertheless meaningless to raise unless we also ask the question of life itself: *Why are we here?* But alas! that question is dismissed as no longer relevant in an academically sophisticated culture. Is this not, then, a self-destructive contradiction for one who debunks the notion of objective morality? Those who reduce the world to merely the physical cheat when they stray into the metaphysical.

In stark distinction, it is here once again that God beckons with His pleas to a morally deaf world. Granted, the questions raised come from two groups. The deep and private pain of those for whom the loss is personal and devastating cannot be simplistically addressed. For them there is One who speaks from a cross. But there is another side to this query, and that is in understanding how and why hatred and murder can be conceived and nurtured in the human heart in the first place.

Again, the very first murder in the Bible did not occur because of two irreconcilable political theories. The murder of a man by his own brother was an act unmistakably borne out of their differing responses to God. God saw Cain's jealousy and hatred toward Abel and warned him to deal with it: "If you do not do what is right, sin is crouching at your door; it desires to have you, but you must rule over it."

There are only two options: either go to God on His terms and find our perfect peace in His acceptance of us, or play God with self-defining morality and kill—becoming as a result restless wanderers, ever running from the voice of our brothers' blood that cries out from the ground. At its core life is sacred and of inestimable value, whether it is the life of a child in the fresh blossom of childhood, or the life of an elderly recluse. Both have one thing in common: they are made in the image of God.

We may try by intellectual duplicity to rearrange the furniture of life and define it only in material terms, but each time we sit back and read of genocide or human trafficking, we shift and turn with revulsion, realizing that there is no harmony in the secular "decor," for the cry within of the sacred cannot be suppressed. That is the reason we scream forth *Why?* at the headlines: we cannot silence the still, small voice inside that speaks of the intrinsic sanctity of life and that it ought not to be violated.

Try as we will, the logical outworking of a denied absolute cannot be escaped. God said it to Cain then and God says it to us now: "If you do not do what is right, sin is crouching at your door; it desires to have you." Cain became a murderer because he willfully refused to worship the living God and chose, by violence, to enthrone himself. This is an aspect of modern society we have grossly underestimated, and in the process we have robbed ourselves of even common sense. God is not only the Creator who defines us philosophically, but God is also the Provider who meets us existentially in our greatest need and gives us the confidence and comfort that we are beloved and not orphaned in this world.

If we are ever to find an answer to the haunting problem of violence, there will need to be a radical shift in our understanding. We must recognize not only the seen, but also the reality of the unseen, for the latter precedes the former. We would do well to take note that long before headlines hit like explosives in our minds, an even greater implosion takes place in the minds and hearts of those who set the news in motion. Human rule cannot deal with that internal devastation, but God can. That unseen war is a spiritual struggle—the choice between turning to God and playing God. For that triumph only God is big enough, and the sooner we realize and acknowledge our need, the closer we will be to moving from the symptomatic rearranging of furniture to the cure of coming home.

REFLECTION QUESTIONS

1. Consider some of the ways we attempt to rearrange the "furniture of life" to suit our view of how the world ought to be.
2. What is the unseen war we struggle with, and what is the solution?

PERSONAL APPLICATION

1. The Scriptures reveal that we are all prone to murder in our hearts. If you have anger and unresolved conflict, ask God to work in you and to bring peace, forgiveness, and healing.
2. Has violence and pain brought home your own need for God? How might you minister to someone in a similar place?

30

THE VALUE OF SOMETHING

Since we have been justified through faith,
we have peace with God through our Lord
Jesus Christ, through whom we have gained
access by faith into this grace in which we now
stand. And we boast in the hope of the glory
of God. Not only so, but we also glory in our
sufferings, because we know that suffering
produces perseverance; perseverance,
character; and character, hope. And hope
does not put us to shame, because God's love
has been poured out into our hearts through
the Holy Spirit, who has been given to us.

ROMANS 5:1–5

During a speaking engagement at an American university, I was handed a question scribbled on a note card from a student who hesitated to come to the microphone. It read, "The state of humankind as we know it is on a serious downward spiral, and from my perspective, it's only getting worse. Do you have any hope in the future of humankind and specifically our generation, and if so, why?"

I was both saddened and heartened to read his question. Overwhelmed by the maze of conflicts facing humanity, this young heart sought a way out. And I believe he represents large numbers of young people in the world. Contrary to the "couldn't care less" image we are often given of university students, he reveals how close to pessimism—and despair—many of them actually are.

Students today are not easily taken in; they do not trust readily. But their questions show a depth and an understanding of our world that is lost in the loud shouts of cultural cynicism or cries of hopeless pessimism. G. K. Chesterton makes a significant point: there is a world of difference between sorrow and pessimism. He explains, "Sorrow is founded on the value of *something*, and pessimism upon the value of *nothing*."[1] In terms of hope for the future, this makes all the difference.

I once had breakfast with an atheist who repeatedly insisted that there was no evidence for God—absolutely none. At one point during our meal he told me how much he loves his wife and painfully recounted the details of her battle with disease. His wife was dying, and he could do nothing. After all the intellectual arguments had run into a headstrong, willful resistance, I asked him why he loved his wife. He stared at me. "Don't you see her as a unique woman of intrinsic value to you?" I asked.

"Yes," he answered.

"But how can she have such value," I replied, "if all life is nothing more than chemicals?"

Suddenly, the conversation took a turn. As we got up from the table, he said, "You just keep doing what you're doing in life. You are bringing back common sense into our heads."

I relate that illustration because I say once again that intrinsic worth and the problem of pain and evil ultimately point to the reality of God's existence. The question then becomes, *Who is God?*

Again, only in Christian theism is love preexistent within the Trinity; thus, love precedes human life and becomes the absolute value for us. This absolute is ultimately found only in God, and in knowing and loving God we work our way through the struggles of pain, knowing of its ultimate connection to evil and its ultimate destruction by the One who is all-good and all-loving—who in fact has given us the very basis for the words *good* and *love* both in concept and in language.

What thoughts occupy my mind as I ponder the world at this present time? Above anything else, I, like the young man from the university, want to believe in hope for the future. I see reason for sorrow, but it is founded on the value of so much. Hope, like character, takes years to build and minutes to shatter. But hope, like character, can also rise beyond the moment to reinvest in what is of ultimate value: an eternal relationship with God.

REFLECTION QUESTIONS

1. What are the many dimensions of hope presented in Romans 5?
2. Explain Chesterton's observation, "Sorrow is founded on the value of *something*."

PERSONAL APPLICATION

1. "Hope, like character, takes years to build and minutes to shatter." How might this perspective direct your steps this week?
2. What are you hopeful about, and where does your hope rest?

31

THE GIFT OF FAITH

Shadrach, Meshach and Abednego replied to him, "King Nebuchadnezzar, we do not need to defend ourselves before you in this matter. If we are thrown into the blazing furnace, the God we serve is able to deliver us from it, and he will deliver us from Your Majesty's hand. But even if he does not, we want you to know, Your Majesty, that we will not serve your gods or worship the image of gold you have set up."

DANIEL 3:16-18

We may be familiar with the concept that faith in God results in works—but we often forget that the reverse is also true. One of the fundamental distinctives of the Hebrew way of thinking that we find in the Scriptures is the understanding that the knowledge of truth comes by obedience. Christians regard *faith* as "belief" or "trust," as the Greek word in the New Testament is often translated. And yet the word for *faith* in the Old Testament is rendered as "faithfulness," suggesting that obedience builds and strengthens one's faith.

A classic demonstration of this principle can be seen in the encounter between God and Moses. When Moses demanded proof that God had indeed called him, God said, "I will be with you. And this will be the sign to you that it is I who have sent you: When you have brought the people out of Egypt, you will worship God on this mountain" (Exodus 3:12). The proof of God's call was after the obedience, not before.

Similarly, Ezekiel, Hosea, and Jonah did not feel like doing what God had asked them to do and questioned Him. In fact, every heartbeat within them was impelling them to do otherwise. Yet God said they were to obey. The remedy was not to do because they felt like doing it, but just to do and their faith would be strengthened.

There are several other instances in the Bible of this urgent struggle to achieve confidence in the wisdom and will of God, even under the impending shadow of death. Think of the prophet Daniel's three friends Shadrach, Meshach, and Abednego facing King Nebuchadnezzar's very real threat to toss them into a fiery furnace if they did not bend to his authority. He was not a charitable man, but they refused to disavow their commitment to God, boldly declaring: "If we are thrown into the blazing furnace, the God we serve is able to deliver us from it. . . . But even if he does not, we want you to know, Your Majesty, that we will not serve your gods or worship the image of gold you have set up." God honored their faith and, in His mercy, delivered them even after they were thrown into the fire. They, in turn, experienced the triumph of faith when they stood their ground.

Being aligned with God's will is no light matter. Nebuchadnezzar had plundered Jerusalem and its temple and took the Jewish people into captivity. He ordered Shadrach, Meshach, Abednego, and Daniel to be instructed in the Babylonian language and philosophy for three years, preparing them to serve in his kingdom. Although Daniel and his friends were subjected to a foreign culture, they held to three principles that allowed them to stand against the powerful forces of their day: they drew a line of resistance, a line of dependence, and a line of confidence in God.

They resisted the temptation to accommodate themselves to the pagan culture of Babylon. They depended upon God and knew where knowledge and education ended, and where trust and wisdom in God began. And they had confidence that God alone was Judge—even as Daniel's own name indicates. (*Daniel* means "God is my judge.")

What happened as a result of their obedience to God? Three pagan kings crossed over from their sides to God's side. Three pagan kings prayed to the God of heaven by the time the book of Daniel ended. The kings steeped the young men in Babylonian philosophy and tried to change their names and worldview. But God's faithful servants ended up changing the kings' allegiances and identities.

Can it still happen? Yes, it can. Certainly it is sometimes easier to resist God's will than to have faith and confidence in Him and in His specific purpose for each one of us. But from the halls of Washington to the boardrooms of Singapore, God is still at work among His people—especially through those who pray.

Prayer teaches us faith—and prayer is hard work. It is not a guarantor of getting what we want or a substitute for action. Rather, it undergirds our action with the strength that makes the difference. Faith is that sublime dependence upon God that even though we may not get what we want, we know and love the One who denies us for His good reason and for our ultimate good. It is the assurance that our Lord superintends our lives in our needs and our dependencies, in our successes and accomplishments. The most significant relationships in life are based on this kind of faith. Such faith faces the defeat of desire with the victory of certainty in the One who is in control.

I would suggest that sometimes we lose our ability to sense God or see Him at work because we choose not to obey Him. The inherent danger within all of us is that no matter what God does, we may wish He had done it differently. The gift of faith is precisely what makes it possible for us to accept that God works in His own way (which is not always our way), in His own time, and for His purpose. It is for us to put aside our doubts and fall in line with God's purpose, always looking forward and waiting patiently for the last link to fall into place. Such are the glorious lessons of faith itself. We do, we obey, we yield, we submit to God even when our natural inclination wants to drag us in the opposite direction.

Only through exercising this kind of faith can the moment be accepted and understood as a small portion of God's bigger story. For some of us that individual story may entail a journey that may be long and hard and arduous, but it will be accomplished one moment at a time, one day at a time, each moment and day undergirded by the strength of the indwelling presence of God. Surely we can rest in Him, confident like Daniel and his friends that the God we serve is able to deliver us—and He will deliver us.

True faith depends not only on God's power but also on His wisdom. The world may caricature it by misunderstanding it. G. K. Chesterton was right when he said, "Faith is always at a disadvantage; it is a perpetually defeated thing which survives all its conquerors."[1]

REFLECTION QUESTIONS

1. What are some biblical examples that support the idea that our knowledge of God's truth comes by obedience?
2. What happened as a result of Daniel and his friends' obedience to God? Is there a contemporary example of their faithfulness that inspires you?

PERSONAL APPLICATION

1. What are the three principles that allowed Daniel and his friends to obey God in a dire situation? Have you drawn these boundary lines as well? How and where?
2. Sometimes we are unable to sense God at work because we choose not to obey Him. Is there an area in your life you need to surrender to God and trust Him to meet you in His way and time?

LIGHT OF THE GOSPEL

"You are the light of the world. A town built on a hill cannot be hidden. Neither do people light a lamp and put it under a bowl. Instead they put it on its stand, and it gives light to everyone in the house. In the same way, let your light shine before others, that they may see your good deeds and glorify your Father in heaven."

MATTHEW 5:14–16

India is the largest movie-producing nation in the world, and to grow up in India is to grow up in a culture where anything on the screen brings a crowd. Romance on the screen was, at the time I was growing up, very typical. Since kissing was not permitted, romantic encounters routinely consisted of a boy-meets-girl scenario that ended with starry-eyed expressions, each chasing the other around trees, with melodramatic music playing. It is best described as grown-ups playing peekaboo in a jungle. Just as the long-awaited moments of embrace came, the scene would change and the audience would applaud.

An Indian comedian who wrote a question-and-answer column in a national film magazine was once asked, "What is the difference between love on the Western screen and love on the Indian screen?" His answer was one word: "Trees." Much has changed in the Indian movie world since, but I shall not chase that issue down.

In the existential questions of our lives and in the struggles of our minds, the trees that separate the worlds of cultures are numerous. Behind all of our superficial distinctives lie the weighty differences: those of values, religion, and worldview. In my work of offering a defense of the Christian faith, God has given me the privilege of speaking on every continent and in dozens of cities, often to those holding a radically different outlook on spiritual matters from my own. I know firsthand that religious issues can be discussed without compromise, yet without animosity, with gentleness, and with respect. While specific beliefs may offend, it is possible to present them without being personally offensive.

I once stayed in Southeast Asia, where I met a wonderful Muslim man. He was the room attendant at my hotel. Every day when he came in to make up my room, he would also make me a cup of tea, and we would talk. He even bought some old Indian movies for me to enjoy. On his day off, he took me sightseeing, and we visited many places of worship. I will never forget him.

On one occasion he invited my wife and me to a lovely dinner at his home. We became very good friends. He knew of my completely different belief to his and would ask me questions. I wish more people showed the kindness he did.

And that is the point I wish to make: we can be worldviews apart without anger or offense. What I believe, I believe very seriously. Indeed, the foundation of my entire life's work is the conviction that Jesus Christ alone is the Way, the Truth, and the Life. Being myself persuaded of this, I am compelled to share that message with others. Yet far more than merely discussing tenets or dogma, I hope to live a life of gentleness and respect, undergirded with love for all people so that the light of the gospel can shine through our differences.

In a world where the trees that separate us are large and discussions of ultimate truth often generate more heat than light, we must seek to come together to consider truth in the open. The barriers to belief may be many. The bridges to every heart ought never to be lost. Then and only then can genuine peace come, made possible by the grace of God.

REFLECTION QUESTIONS

1. Can you think of some cultural differences between you and others that tend to divide when issues of values and religion are discussed?
2. According to 1 Peter 3:15, what two elements are critical when we engage others who may be worldviews apart from us?

PERSONAL APPLICATION

1. Do you know someone whose culture and worldview are radically different from yours? Consider how your friendship and kindness could be a bridge to reveal the love of Christ.
2. The tenets of the Christian faith are essential, but if we have not love, we are "clanging cymbals" (see 1 Corinthians 13). Learning to love involves a lifetime, but what could you do today to grow in love and shine the light of the gospel?

33

SHOW US THE FATHER

Philip said, "Lord, show us the Father
and that will be enough for us."
Jesus answered: "Don't you know me, Philip,
even after I have been among you such a long
time? Anyone who has seen me has seen the
Father. How can you say, 'Show us the Father'?
Don't you believe that I am in the Father, and
that the Father is in me? The words I say to you
I do not speak on my own authority. Rather, it is
the Father, living in me, who is doing his work."

JOHN 14:8-10

At a Christmas Eve service we attended one year, a short play was featured. It was a monologue by Joseph as, moments after the birth of Jesus, he held the little one in his arms and spoke to Him. He looked into the face of the baby and, with all the musings of a new father, playfully talked about His resemblance to His mother. But then he paused and in all seriousness whispered, "I wonder what Your Father looks like." One could sense that the hundreds in the audience echoed those sentiments.

Throughout history artists, writers, musicians, scholars, and all who have read the life of Jesus have wondered what He looked like. Interestingly enough, those who actually saw Him took the search a step further: "Show us the Father," they said. Indeed, one of the first questions the disciples asked of Jesus was, "Where do you live?" (Sheer humor would have wanted Him to respond, "You'd never believe Me if I told you!") Whether the Jesus of history or God the Creator, many have wondered what He looked like.

Saint Augustine wrote of a Faustian-type encounter when a momentary delight was offered to him. The only condition was that he would forfeit the pleasure of ever seeing God. He concluded without hesitation: "No pleasure is worth that loss."

In the Father's grace and wisdom, God has blessed us with intellects and senses that long to see, to hear, and to know Him. At the same time, God has allowed our imaginations both liberty and limitation. God cautioned us never to make a graven image. It bears reminding that though we exalt a person by carving him or her in stone or painting on canvas, attempting the same for God, we are warned, only reduces God. Circumscribing God is fraught with the peril of our own prejudice, to say nothing of its being contradictory.

The Scriptures tell us little about the physical appearance of Jesus. We shall all, therefore, have to await the day when "every eye will see him." But where physical features have been guardedly presented, and with reason, the Scriptures are profuse in describing for us God's person, God's character, and His loving revelation to us in the person of Jesus. In mining the wealth of that content, we come to understand how profoundly God has responded to the cry of the human heart, *Who are You, God?* This ought to be the paramount quest of every man, woman, and child, because from that knowledge flows every other answer to the cries of the heart and mind.

REFLECTION QUESTIONS

1. What are some characteristics of God the Father found in the Scriptures?
2. Jesus said, "Anyone who has seen me has seen the Father." How does Jesus "show us the Father"?

PERSONAL APPLICATION

1. For some, the fatherhood of God elicits negative associations with an earthly father or parent. What aspect of God's character do you most need to believe? His faithfulness, His love, His protection, His compassion?
2. Consider how the answer to *Who are You, God?* responds to the deepest needs of your heart and mind. Ask God to reveal Himself today in your place of need.

34

A TASTE OF WORSHIP

Is anyone among you in trouble? Let them
pray. Is anyone happy? Let them sing songs
of praise. Is anyone among you sick? Let
them call the elders of the church to pray
over them and anoint them with oil in the
name of the Lord. And the prayer offered
in faith will make the sick person well; the
Lord will raise them up. If they have sinned,
they will be forgiven. Therefore confess your
sins to each other and pray for each other
so that you may be healed. The prayer of a
righteous person is powerful and effective.

JAMES 5:13-16

Years ago, I read a definition of worship that to this day rings with clear and magnificent terms. The definition comes from the famed archbishop William Temple: "Worship is the submission of all of our nature to God. It is the quickening of the conscience by his holiness; the nourishment of mind with his truth; the purifying of imagination by his beauty; the opening of the heart to his love; the surrender of will to his purpose—all this gathered up in adoration, the most selfless emotion of which our nature is capable."[1]

The more I have thought of that definition, the more I am convinced that if worship is practiced with integrity in the community of God's people, worship may be the most powerful evangel for this postmodern culture of ours. It is imperative that in planning the worship services, the pastor and church leaders give careful attention to every element and make sure that the worship retains both integrity and purpose. People come to church generally beaten down by the world of deceit, distraction, and demand. There is an extraction of emotional and spiritual energy that brings them "on empty" into the community. The minister and worship leaders' tasks are to so prepare during the week that they will be instruments of replenishment and fresh energy of soul.

Of course, even being in the presence of fellow believers in worship is a restorer of spiritual hope. We so underestimate the power of a people in one mind and with one commitment. Likewise, as I have suggested before, prayer can so touch a hungry heart that it can rescue a sliding foot in a treacherous time.

A few years ago, a few of my colleagues and I were in a country dominated for decades by Marxism. Before we began our meetings, we were invited to a dinner hosted by some common friends, all of whom were skeptics and, for all practical purposes, atheists. The evening was full of questions, posed principally by a notable theoretical physicist. There were also others who represented different elements of power within that society. As the night wore on, we got the feeling that the questions had gone on long enough and we were possibly going in circles.

At that point, I asked if we could have a word of prayer with them, for them, and for the country before we bade them good-bye. There was a silence of consternation, an obvious hesitancy, and then one said, "Of course."

So, we did just that—we prayed. In this large dining room of historic import to them, with all the memories of secular power plastered within those walls, the prayer brought a sobering silence that we were all in the presence of Someone greater than us. When we finished, every eye was moist and nothing was said. They hugged us and thanked us, with emotion written all over their faces.

The next day when we met them, one of them said to me, "We did not go back to our rooms last night till it was early morning. In fact, I stayed in my hotel lobby most of the night talking further. Then I went back to my room and gave my life to Jesus Christ."

I firmly believe that it was prayer that gave them a hint of the taste of what worship is all about. Their hearts had never experienced it.

Over the years I have discovered that praying with people can sometimes do more for them than preaching to them. Prayer draws the heart away from one's own dependence to leaning on the sovereign God. The burden is often lifted instantly, especially when one hears someone pray who firmly believes in the love and abiding presence of God. To a person in need, pat answers don't change the mind; prayer does.

REFLECTION QUESTIONS

1. According to William Temple (and Scripture), what is worship?
2. Consider the ways we might respond to prayer and preaching when we are on the receiving end, listening.

PERSONAL APPLICATION

1. Prayer is a taste of worship, drawing us into intimacy with God. Give thanks to God for the gift of prayer and the privilege to enjoy His fellowship.
2. Is there a burden you might help lighten today by interceding for someone? Can you ask someone to do the same for you?

35

LIVING TEMPLES

Flee from sexual immorality. All other sins a
person commits are outside the body, but
whoever sins sexually, sins against their own
body. Do you not know that your bodies
are temples of the Holy Spirit, who is in you,
whom you have received from God? You are
not your own; you were bought at a price.
Therefore honor God with your bodies.

1 CORINTHIANS 6:18-20

In the late 1970s, sociologist Daniel Bell defined *culture* as "the effort to provide a coherent set of answers to the existential predicaments that confront all human beings in the passage of their lives."[1] From what we cherish to what we abhor, from how we live to how we die, from what is sacred to what is profane, in each decision we try to make sense out of our lives. And culture is that sort of glue that holds our common values together.

Strangely, nowadays to understand culture even in those terms may well be outdated. I recall, for example, lecturing at a university when a student stormed up to the microphone and bellowed, "Who told you culture is a search for coherence? Where do you get that idea from? This idea of coherence is a Western idea."

Rather surprised, I replied by reminding her that all I had done was present a sociologist's definition. "Ah! Words! Just words!" she shouted back.

"Let me ask you this then," I said. "Do you want my answer to be coherent?"

At that moment, laughter rippled through the auditorium. She herself was stymied for a few moments. "But that's language, isn't it?" she retorted.

So I asked her if language had anything to do with reality. "Don't words refer to something? If you are seeking an intelligible answer from me, mustn't there be correspondence between my words and reality? How then can this basic requirement be met in our culture?"

Of course, this student is only reflecting the spirit of thought among us today—no truth, no meaning, no certainty. We now hear that language is detached from reality and truth is detached from meaning. What we are left with is a way of thinking basically shaped by our appetites and by our proclivities, which is how life has become defined by our untamed passions. Hence, incoherence is now normal.

In a staggering contrast, Scripture pleads that our lives were meant to be temples of the living God: "Do you not know that your bodies are temples of the Holy Spirit, who is in you, whom you have received from God?" (1 Corinthians 6:19).

Only when we understand what it means for our bodies to be the temple of God can we understand what living means and how coherence is born. For you see, life is not made sacred by going to a place of worship; life already is sacred and that is why it moves us to a place of worship. In this sense, wherever you are, you cannot leave without the temple. Profane it and reap incoherence; keep it sacred and harmony ensues.

Even Jesus spoke of His body as the temple of God (see John 2:19–21). If we are in Christ, we are not our own. We have been bought with His precious blood and called as His church "the body of Christ": "Now you are the body of Christ, and each one of you is a part of it" (1 Corinthians 12:27). What a stunning and precious truth! May our whole selves reflect God's purpose for our lives. In this truth we will find true coherence and peace.

REFLECTION QUESTIONS

1. What is the function of a temple? What descriptions come to mind when you think of a temple?
2. Read 1 Corinthians 1. In what ways is the church understood to be the body of Christ?

PERSONAL APPLICATION

1. What thoughts and feelings are evoked by the truth that our bodies are the very temples of God, where His Spirit resides? How might you live in light of this awareness today?
2. "You are not your own; you were bought at a price." You belong to God—you are a child of God! Take time to praise God for "his indescribable gift" (2 Corinthians 9:15).

36

A BEACON OF HOPE

In the year that King Uzziah died, I saw the
Lord, high and exalted, seated on a throne; and
the train of his robe filled the temple. Above
him were seraphim . . . calling to one another:

"Holy, holy, holy is the Lord Almighty;
the whole earth is full of his glory."

At the sound of their voices the doorposts and
thresholds shook and the temple was filled with smoke.
"Woe to me!" I cried. "I am ruined! For I am a
man of unclean lips . . . and my eyes have seen
the King, the Lord Almighty."

ISAIAH 6:1–5

The story is told of a cynic sitting under a nut tree, carrying on a jesting monologue with God. His grounds for complaint lay in what he considered to be an obvious failure on the part of God to go by the book on structural design. "Lord," he said, "how is it that you made such a large and sturdy tree to hold such tiny, almost weightless nuts? And yet you made small, tender plants to hold such large and weighty watermelons!"

As he chuckled at the folly of such disproportion in God's mindless universe, a nut suddenly fell on his head. After a stunned pause, he muttered, "Thank God that wasn't a watermelon!"

Justifiable worldviews must have explanatory power of the undeniable realities of life. As Christians who affirm the existence of a loving and all-wise God, we long to be a beacon of hope in our world and to see the light of God's Word soften the cynic and atheist alike. Yet if we are honest, sometimes we too struggle to come to terms with God's world and His sovereign design; this is especially true in seasons of suffering and confusion.

Remember Job? He had become weary of his pain and sought a just answer for it. He built his argument to God on the fact that he needed to know what was going on, because only on the basis of that knowledge could his confusion and suffering be dissipated. But God then broke His silence, challenging Job's very assumptions and reminding him that there was an awful lot he did not know but had just accepted and believed by inference. Notwithstanding the proverbial cynic under a nut tree, the argument from design is the very approach God used with Job. He reminded Job as a first step, and only that, that there were a thousand and one things he did not fully understand but had just taken for granted. In the light of God's presence, Job was dumbfounded and confessed, "I am unworthy—how can I reply to you? . . . Surely I spoke of things I did not understand, things too wonderful for me to know" (Job 40:4, 42:3).

Likewise, the prophet Isaiah described his awestricken state when God revealed Himself to him. Isaiah, a morally good man, nevertheless fell on his face and immediately sensed that he was unfit to be in God's presence. He was not just in the presence of someone better than he was. He was in the presence of the One by whom and because of whom all purity finds its point of reference. That is why he was speechless.

God is not merely good. God is holy. He is the transcendent Source of goodness: not merely "better" in a hierarchy of choices but rather the very basis from which all differences are made. He dwells in ineffable light. Moral categories, for us, often move in comparisons and hierarchies. We talk in terms of judging or feeling that one thing is better than another. Our culture is more advanced morally than someone else's culture, at least so we may think. However, God's existence changes those categories and moves us to recognize the very essence of what the word *goodness* is based upon.

This difference is what makes the argument almost impossible for a skeptic to grasp. Holiness is not merely goodness. "Why did God not create us to choose only good?" "Why do bad things happen to good people?" The reality is that the opposite of evil, in degree, may be goodness. But the opposite of absolute evil, in kind, is absolute holiness. In the biblical context, the idea of holiness is the tremendous *otherness* of God Himself. God does not just reveal Himself as good; He reveals Himself as holy.

There is no contradiction in Him. He can never self-destruct. He can never not be. He exists eternally and in a sublime purity that transcends a hierarchy of categories. As human beings we love the concept of holiness when we are in the right, but we are often reticent to apply it when we are wrong and brought under the stark scrutiny of its light.

You see, the problem of evil begins with me. The darkness is within.

Yet Jesus' answer, for instance, to the question of the blind man in John 9 brings us extraordinary power and hope. People wanted to know, why was he born this way? Jesus responded that the man's blindness was due neither to the sin of the man nor of his parents, but so that the glory of God might be displayed. The lesson is drastic, the message profound. Physical darkness has physical consequences and leaves a person bereft of seeing physical reality. It is a tragedy— but nowhere near the tragic devastation of spiritual blindness. The healing of that man's blindness by Jesus was intended to draw those spiritually blind to seek His healing of their souls.

When Beethoven, though deaf, could see the exhilarating response of the people to his composition, he outwardly resonated with what his inner being prompted. He could not hear his music, but he sensed the harmony for which he longed in expression. So it is with us. We know on the inside how impoverished we are and for what we long. That ought to prompt us to the riches that only God in Christ is able to give to us.

Only when we surrender to the light of God's truth in our own lives are we enabled to truly see and then be a beacon of hope and healing in our dark world. Truthfulness in the heart precedes truth in the objective realm. The problem of evil has ultimately one source: it is the resistance to God's holiness that enshrouds all of creation. And there is ultimately only one hope for life: that is through the glorious display of God at work within a human soul. That transformation tenderizes the heart to become part of the solution and not part of the problem. Such transformation begins at the foot of the cross.

REFLECTION QUESTIONS

1. God is not merely good, and His holiness is not merely goodness. Explain.
2. How does Scripture define *holiness*? What is meant by *otherness*?

PERSONAL APPLICATION

1. Read Isaiah 6 and/or Revelation 4. How is God's holiness linked with worship and intimacy with Him?
2. How can you be a beacon of God's hope in your sphere of influence this week?

37

THE BOOKS WE READ

As for you, continue in what you have learned and have become convinced of, because you know those from whom you learned it, and how from infancy you have known the Holy Scriptures, which are able to make you wise for salvation through faith in Christ Jesus. All Scripture is God-breathed and is useful for teaching, rebuking, correcting and training in righteousness, so that the servant of God may be thoroughly equipped for every good work.

2 TIMOTHY 3:14–17

My father-in-law and I often spoke wistfully about fine used bookstores that we had visited. He told one story, however, that has all the others soundly beaten.

He was in a sophisticated bookstore in Toronto that caters to the academic community, a bookstore rich in classical tradition. Suddenly, in came a roughshod man in greasy overalls, who bellowed to the owner, "How much does it cost to buy 128 feet of books?"

Obviously bewildered by this request, for never before had he sold scholarly works by the foot, the owner replied, "Uh . . . what exactly did you have in mind?" Meanwhile every customer within earshot had paused from reading, ears pinned for some new enlightenment.

It turns out the buyer had been sent by a group of trade union leaders who were hosting their educated counterparts in management in an effort to break a deadlock in some highly volatile negotiations. So, the union leaders decided to decorate their offices with the length of books. Why? To convey the intimidating air of being ideological heavyweights, and to terrify the opposition!

Amusing story, is it not?

Solomon reminds us that there is nothing new under the sun, and so I suspect that this was not the first such scenario in history. After all, jockeying for literary superiority is as old as the printed page. No doubt many of us have had occasion to purchase classics that have served ulterior purposes—giving the appearance that we are wise.

It is said that a lady once wrote to the famed writer A. W. Tozer and thanked him for his Christian journal, commenting that it perfectly fit her birdcage! Groucho Marx once responded to an author, "From the moment I picked your book up until I laid it down, I was convulsed with laughter. Someday I intend reading it."

I suspect there are books like that in your own experience that, while not provoking laughter, have never entered the mind. One critic said of the late Stephen Hawking's *A Brief History of Time,* which shattered all records on the bestseller list in the United Kingdom, that it would be the most-bought and least-read book in recent memory.

And yet who of us has not entered another world or gained a life-changing insight just from reading a book? Friends, don't take the power of reading for granted. I am absolutely convinced that the books you and I read possibly help mold our lives more purposefully— and eternally, I might add—than we ever realize.

As King Solomon said, "Of making many books there is no end," but finding wisdom "preserves the lives of its possessors" (Ecclesiastes 12:12 NKJV; 7:12 NASB). And to that I would say only the book of all books, the Bible, stands above all others, "for the word of God is alive and active. Sharper than any double-edged sword, it penetrates even to dividing soul and spirit, joints and marrow; it judges the thoughts and attitudes of the heart" (Hebrews 4:12). The regenerative power of the Word is why the Bible will outlive its pallbearers and continue to transform hearts and minds in every culture and every generation.

REFLECTION QUESTIONS

1. Consider the ways being well read—or having an office filled with books—can be intimidating. How might it be less so?
2. How does culture, especially in a social media era, encourage us to misuse knowledge and literacy to gain an edge or promote a certain image of ourselves?

PERSONAL APPLICATION

1. Which books have made the most impact on you? How and why do you think they have been so life-defining?
2. What do the passages from 2 Timothy 3 and Hebrews 4 tell you about the Word of God and its effects? How has reading Scripture changed you?

38

RIGHT WHERE WE ARE WRONG

Don't let anyone look down on you
because you are young, but set an example
for the believers in speech, in conduct,
in love, in faith and in purity. . . .
Be diligent in these matters; give yourself
wholly to them, so that everyone may see
your progress. Watch your life and doctrine
closely. Persevere in them, because if you do,
you will save both yourself and your hearers.

1 TIMOTHY 4:12, 15–16

Plato once remarked that he was grateful to be born a Greek and not a barbarian, a free man and not a slave, a man and not a woman, and most of all, to have been born in the age of Socrates.

Do you feel, like I, a twinge of discomfort in hearing this? For his sentiment reveals two of our perennial struggles: to find a philosophy by which to live and to correct the prejudices with which we live. One would think the connection between the two is too obvious to miss and the fact that one informs the other ought to stare each of us in the face. Yet if history has taught us anything, it is that we learn very little from the past, and we do not pause either to justify what we believe or to make sure that doctrine and conduct have a life-giving connection. That which God has joined together let no person put asunder.

I was once asked to speak at a conference on ethics at a certain university I'll leave unnamed. I dared to present the bankruptcy of humanistic theories both rationally and practically and contrasted them with the biblical basis for ethics. After the presentation, there was silence for a long while. Then one professor said to me, "All this theory sounds good, but the real question is, how do I get my students to be ethical, to not cheat on their exams, to tell the truth?"

I was thrilled at the question for, in fact, that was the point of the whole talk. But I was not prepared for what followed.

After the question-and-answer session, a student came up and presented me with a real dilemma. Here's what she said: "I was asked to come to your lecture today by my professor. The expectation was that I would disagree with you and so write a paper saying that. But after listening to your talk, I found myself agreeing with you and now have a serious problem. If I write in defense of your position, I will probably be given a very low grade, if not failed. On the other hand, she said if I disagree with you I am sure to get a high grade. My problem is the challenge to tell the truth and risk failure."

Rather puzzled, I looked at her and I said, "Did your professor come to the forum?"

There was silence and then came the answer. "Yes," she said, rather softly.

"Who was it?" I asked.

"The one who asked you the question about getting away from the theory to the bottom line of how to get students to not cheat and to tell the truth."

Do you believe that? I was dumbfounded. Is there any doubt why many a college student has failed to link thought with life and lives as a bundle of contradictions when taught by ethicists who have severed the heart from the head and still hope to live?

To this end Paul warned Timothy to cherish the Scripture, for it made him "wise unto salvation" (2 Timothy 3:15 KJV) and to "watch [his] life and doctrine closely" (1 Timothy 4:16). The Scriptures are meaningful and personal because they are true, and not true just because we can wrest them to advantage or manipulate them into personal meaning. Meaning and application can be prostituted at the altar of self-gratification, but truth will stand in history when all human dissenters have said their last.

G. K. Chesterton said it well: "We do not really want a religion that is right where we are right. What we want is a religion that is right where we are wrong."[1] Only the Word of God provides that corrective. That warning comes to both skeptic and believer alike.

You see, God corrects us not because of appearances but because of His character. Goodness points us not to theory but to the purpose of life.

REFLECTION QUESTIONS

1. Consider how the professor's question belied her true intentions. What did she really want?
2. Right doctrine and conduct don't save us, so what does Paul mean when he urges Timothy, "Persevere in them, because if you do, you will save both yourself and your hearers"?

PERSONAL APPLICATION

1. When are you prone to sever the heart from the head— perhaps at the prospect of pleasure and for fear of missing out? Ask God to reveal to you habits of the heart that need His corrective grace.
2. Have you been in a situation similar to the student's? What did you do, or how would you conduct yourself now?

39

PORTRAIT OF A SOUL

"Come now, let us settle the matter,"
says the Lᴏʀᴅ.
"Though your sins are like scarlet,
they shall be as white as snow;
though they are red as crimson,
they shall be like wool.
If you are willing and obedient,
you will eat the good things of the land;
but if you resist and rebel,
you will be devoured by the sword."
For the mouth of the Lᴏʀᴅ has spoken.

ISAIAH 1:18–20

In the novel *The Picture of Dorian Gray,* Oscar Wilde describes an exceptionally handsome young man so captivating that he drew the awestricken adulation of a great artist. The artist asked him to be the subject of a portrait, for he had never seen a face so attractive and so pure. When the painting was completed, young Dorian became so enraptured by his own looks that he wistfully intoned how wonderful it would be if he could live any way he pleased but that no disfigurement of a lawless lifestyle would mar the picture of his own countenance. If only the portrait would grow old and he himself could remain unscathed by time and way of life. In Faustian style, he was willing to trade his soul for that wish.

One day, alone and pensive, Dorian went up to the attic and uncovered the portrait that he had kept hidden for so many years, only to be shocked by what he saw. Horror, hideousness, and blood marred the portrait.

The charade came to an end when the artist himself saw the picture. It told the story. He pled with Dorian to come clean, saying, "Does it not say somewhere, 'Though your sins be as scarlet, yet I will make them white as snow'?" But in a fit of rage to silence this voice of conscience, Dorian grabbed a knife and killed the artist.

There was now only one thing left for him to do; he took the knife to remove the only visible reminder of his wicked life. But the moment he thrust the blade into the canvas, the portrait returned to its pristine beauty, while Dorian lay stabbed to death on the floor. The ravages that had marred the picture now so disfigured him that even his servants could no longer recognize him.

What a brilliant illustration of how a soul, though invisible, can nonetheless be tarnished. I wonder, if there were to be a portrait of my soul or yours, how would it best be depicted? Does not the conscience sting when we think in these terms? Though we have engineered many ways of avoiding physical consequences, how does one cleanse the soul?

Today we find a limitless capacity to raise the question of evil as we see it outside ourselves, but often we hold an equal unwillingness to address the evil within us. I once sat on the top floor of a huge corporate building owned by a very successful businessman. Our entire conversation revolved around his reason for unbelief: that there was so much darkness and corruption in this world and a seemingly silent God. Suddenly interrupting the dialogue, a friend of mine said to him, "Since evil troubles you so much, I would be curious to know what you have done with the evil you see within you." There was red-faced silence.

We too face Dorian Gray's predicament. Sooner or later, a duplicitous life reveals the cost. The soul is not forever invisible. But there is One who can cleanse and restore us. The Christian worldview gives us extraordinary insight into this subject of our soul-struggle, as God deals with the heart of the issue one life at a time. Indeed, in the words of the prophet Isaiah to which Oscar Wilde alluded: "Come now, and let us reason together, saith the LORD: though your sins be as scarlet, they shall be as white as snow; though they be red like crimson, they shall be as wool" (KJV).

God upholds the solution, asking only that we come "willing and obedient" and that we don't "resist and rebel" (Isaiah 1:20). So come, willingly and obediently, and find God's rejoinder to the marred portraits within. The greatest Artist of all speaks even today.

REFLECTION QUESTIONS

1. What perspective and reasoning would drive a person to forfeit his or her life and commitments for the sake of pleasure and limitless freedom?
2. How did the businessman betray his own heart? Why must the question of evil first begin with the one asking it?

PERSONAL APPLICATION

1. If there were a portrait of your soul, what would it look like after God's brushstrokes of grace and forgiveness?
2. How do you want to be remembered? Are you investing in this legacy in your relationships, work, and ministry?

40

REGENERATIVE POWER

We also have the prophetic message as something completely reliable, and you will do well to pay attention to it, as to a light shining in a dark place, until the day dawns and the morning star rises in your hearts. Above all, you must understand that no prophecy of Scripture came about by the prophet's own interpretation of things. For prophecy never had its origin in the human will, but prophets, though human, spoke from God as they were carried along by the Holy Spirit.

2 PETER 1:19-21

Some years ago I read a powerful book by the famed theologian Carl F. H. Henry entitled *The Christian Mindset in a Secular Society.* The book was quite prophetic, for it set forth plainly where the lines of a cultural battle were being drawn and how far-reaching would be the fallout.

Two ideas that he juxtaposed immediately caught my attention. The first was that "biblical truth, transcultural as it is, has an indispensable message for modern man."[1] The statement is a very logical conclusion for anyone with a high view of Scripture. But then came the blunt portrayal of the contemporary scene in its relentless emasculation of truth, the hallmark of modern humanity. Carl Henry referred to this generation as "intellectually uncapped, morally unzipped and volitionally uncurbed."[2]

This disturbing reality was driven home to me in a story relayed by a friend, a professional actor who dramatically narrates Scripture word for word. Describing his last performance at a university, he said he had experienced something thoroughly unnerving. As he enacted the anguish of Christ on the way to death, students laughed through the presentation, mocking the pathos. This would never have happened in a Hindu or Buddhist context, where reverence is shown for anything spiritual, even if it is not part of their creed. Clearly our context is different.

How then does one communicate to people who have bought into such a mind-set as Henry describes, who openly reject ultimate authority and ridicule the sacred? The answer is not simple, but we rob ourselves if we think it is therefore impossible.

First, let us be absolutely certain that every generation at some time has in its own way resisted the truth that God has proclaimed. In Matthew 11, Jesus compared His own generation to children in a marketplace crying out,

> "We played the pipe for you,
>> and you did not dance;
> we sang a dirge,
>> and you did not mourn." (v. 17)

They wanted John the Baptist to dance because they considered his message—the demands of the law—too somber. On the other hand, when Jesus came with the message of grace and freedom, they wanted Him to mourn because it was too merciful. Any message that threatens our autonomy is automatically rejected, no matter what it is.

Second, as cultural fads ebb and flow, the inescapable truth emerges that century after century the power of God's written Word has surpassed, and will continue to surpass, the exhilarations of momentary experience, which are conceived and die in an instant. We tenderly set a halo on the forehead of feeling or miracle, but in times of greatest loss it is the written Word, the embodied Word, that carries us through, not feeling.

The apostle Peter reminds us of this very truth. We must remember that this is the same Peter who experienced the ecstasy of the transfiguration—a sight that caused him to plead that he and those with him be permitted to bask permanently in its afterglow. It is Peter who, contrasting the temporariness of that experience with the eternal and unfading brilliance of the Word, said, "We have also a more sure word of prophecy" (2 Peter 1:19 KJV). Inscripturation (the preservation of the written word) has a present and eternal point of reference, transcending mere flashes of feeling or of the miraculous.

Over the span of life, the Word can be tested time and time again, and its truths will stand tall as our culture's fascination with the subjective proves itself to be hollow and false. By contrast, the biblical documents have withstood the most scrutinizing analysis ever imposed upon any manuscript and have emerged with compelling authenticity and authority. No other ancient literature demonstrates such a high degree of accuracy.

Not only does the Word come persuasively inscribed on paper, but also the effectual power of the Word is evidenced when that inscription, proclaimed through the Spirit, embodied in Christ Jesus, brings life-changing conviction with it. Let us never forget the very incarnation itself, where the Word became flesh and came to dwell among us. The transformation that comes as a result of this personal touch is what regeneration is all about, when the letter of the Word and the Word as Christ Himself are written on the heart of the hearer.

The Scriptures, the touch, the presence, and the love of Christ lived out—these combined become the sword of the Spirit to break down the armored resistance of a culture at war with His truth. For ultimately, all pursuits apart from God lead to alienation and loneliness that only the touch of Christ can resolve.

The Christian, therefore, stands in the position to proclaim and live the truth that reaches the mind, stirs the heart, and purifies the imagination. The regenerative power of the Word is what makes it indispensable to every culture and every generation in every century. That's why we are told that we don't live by bread alone, but by every word that proceeds from the mouth of God.

REFLECTION QUESTIONS

1. Imagine a generation that is "intellectually uncapped, morally unzippered and volitionally uncurbed." Consider how the beauty and truth of the gospel can transform people bearing each of these descriptions.
2. What elements become the sword of the Spirit to break down the armored resistance of a culture at war with God's truth?

PERSONAL APPLICATION

1. How did the regenerative power of the Scriptures and the love of Christ first change your life? Thank God for the gracious work He has done and is doing in your life.
2. God's Word is "a light shining in a dark place." Read 1 John 3:19–22 and invite God's Word, Christ Himself, to shine His light and love in every corner of your life.

41

MAN OF SORROWS

He was despised and rejected by mankind,
a man of suffering, and familiar with pain.
Like one from whom people hide their faces
he was despised, and we held him in low esteem.
Surely he took up our pain
and bore our suffering,
yet we considered him punished by God,
stricken by him, and afflicted. . . .
We all, like sheep, have gone astray,
each of us has turned to our own way;
and the Lord has laid on him
the iniquity of us all.

ISAIAH 53:3–4, 6

P rosperity, pleasure and success, may be rough of grain and common in fibre, but sorrow is the most sensitive of all created things."[1] Those are the words of the famed pleasure seeker Oscar Wilde. In his *De Profundis*, written in prison, he spoke with profound earnestness about how much sorrow had taught him. He went on to add, "Where there is sorrow there is holy ground. Some day people will realise what that means. They will know nothing of life till they do."[2]

As I reflect on those words, I take note first of the one who wrote them. A life of pain was the furthest thing from Oscar Wilde's mind when he made his choices. In that sense, none of us ever really chooses sorrow. But I take note of something else in his words: his claim is bold. He is not merely confessing an idea written across his worldview, but one he insists is written across the world. Sorrow is holy ground, he says, and those who do not learn to walk there know nothing of what living means.

What he means at the very least is that some of life's most sacred truths are learned in the midst of sorrow. He learned, for example, that raw, unadulterated pleasure for pleasure's sake is never a fulfilling pleasure. Violation of the sacred in the pursuit of happiness is not truly a source of happiness. In fact, it kills happiness because it can run roughshod over many a victim. Pleasure that profanes is pleasure that destroys.

Sorrow, on the other hand, while never pursued, comes into one's life and compels us to see our own finitude and frailty. It demands of us seriousness and tenderness if we are to live life the way it is meant to be lived. One of the most important things sorrow does is to show us what it needs and responds to. Wilde said it himself: sorrow "is a wound that bleeds when any hand but that of love touches it, and even then must bleed again, though not in pain."[3]

Of all the descriptions given about Jesus, there is one that unabashedly stands out to confront us. It is a description uttered by the prophet Isaiah, prodding mind and heart at once:

> He was despised and rejected by mankind,
>   a man of suffering, and familiar with pain.
> Like one from whom people hide their faces
>   he was despised, and we held him in low esteem.
> Surely he took up our pain and bore our suffering,
>   yet we considered him punished by God,
>   stricken by him, and afflicted.

Whether holding glimpses of global suffering or personal pain and loss, Isaiah offers a fitting description to reflect upon. Indeed, he goes on to prophesy in verse 5 of Jesus,

> But he was pierced for our transgressions,
>   he was crushed for our iniquities;
> the punishment that brought us peace was on him,
>   and by his wounds we are healed.

Maybe you are at a time in your life when hurt is writ large upon your thoughts. Jesus is not unacquainted with your pain. In fact, He draws near particularly with a hand of love. Your wound may still bleed for a while to remind you of your weakness. But He can help carry the pain to carry you in strength. This could indeed be holy ground for you. It most certainly was for Him.

REFLECTION QUESTIONS

1. What does it mean to say that sorrow is holy ground?
2. What does the prophet Isaiah tell us about the person and ministry of Jesus and the response He would encounter during His life on earth?

PERSONAL APPLICATION

1. Have you found that life's most sacred truths are learned in the midst of sorrow? How might this perspective change your understanding of suffering or minister to someone you love?
2. Spend time praying for Jesus' peace and healing in your life and for others in need.

42

CASTING STONES

When they kept on questioning him, he . . .
said to them, "Let any one of you who is
without sin be the first to throw a stone at
her." Again he stooped down and wrote on
the ground. At this, those who heard began
to go away one at a time, the older ones first,
until only Jesus was left. . . . "Woman, where
are they? Has no one condemned you?"

"No one, sir," she said.

"Then neither do I condemn you," Jesus
declared. "Go now and leave your life of sin."

JOHN 8:7-11

L et him who is without sin . . . cast the first stone." This thought is often given as rationale for casting any type of public moralizing aside. Evidently, we cannot completely shake off our bequest from a Christian worldview. Ironically, this moral conviction is often given with the reminder that all morality is a private matter and not for public enforcement. But if all moral convictions are a private matter, why is this very conviction itself not kept private too? Why is it publicly enjoined?

When I ask citers of this verse from John 8 if they are aware of the context in which these words were uttered, they often don't know. One said it had to do with the woman in adultery. I asked if he was aware of what prompted Jesus' imperative and to whom He aimed those words. There was silence. Significantly, the entire confrontation came about because the Pharisees were seeking to trap Jesus into either explicitly defending the law of Moses or implicitly overruling it. The whole scenario was a ploy, not to seek out the truth of a moral law, but to trap Jesus.

Fascinatingly, Jesus exposed their own spiritual bankruptcy by showing them that at the heart of the law is God's very character. That is, there is a spiritual essence that precedes moral injunctions. So when we vociferously demand that only the one without sin may cast the first stone, we also need to grant credence to God's character in numerous other pronouncements.

But for some, sin is not even a viable category. This selective use of Scripture is the very game the questioners of Jesus were playing. When the law is quoted while the reality of sin is denied, self-aggrandizing motives can override character. Thus, in our spiritually amputated world, the art of obscuring truth has become a science in courtroom and political theatrics.

Herein lies what I believe is the crucial death of our characters. There is no transcendent context within which to discuss moral theory. Just as words, in order to have meaning, must point beyond themselves to a commonly understood real existence, so also must reality point beyond itself to a commonly accepted essence. Otherwise reality has no moral quotient and moral meaning dissolves into the subjective, rendering it beyond debate. Only the transcendent can unchangingly provide fixed moral worth.

But this death of the transcendent comes with a two-edged sword, both for the skeptic and the Christian alike. Yes, the law has moral value, but not as a means for shrewd lawyers to play deadly word games, minimize immorality, and kill the truth. At the same time the law has spiritual value so that we do not destroy the truly repentant individual. The grace of God abounds to the worst in our midst. Hidden in the odious nature of our failures is the scandalous secret of God's forgiveness. When the prodigal returned, the anger he faced was not from his father but from his older brother, who failed to understand the marvelous grace of his father.

Throughout history, God's way of dealing with the reckless has disclosed how dramatic are His ways. We must allow for such possibilities. "This son of mine was dead and is alive again," shouted the prodigal's father (Luke 15:24). Death lay in the wanderings of the passions and the seriousness of wrongdoing. Life was spelled in true repentance to return and "sin no more." But let us take note: forgiveness is offered in full recognition of the heinousness of what is being forgiven.

On the contrary, when words, consequences, and transcendent contexts have died, a pigsty awaits. Only if we remember our Father's address can we know where to return for forgiveness and love. But if we insist upon arguing as quick-witted political power-mongers or legal wordsmiths with no spiritual context, we may kill both law and love. This, I am afraid, is the abyss over which we often hover.

Yet I am confident that as precipitous as the edge seems, God has always been in the business of rescue. The truth is that as human beings we all fall short. Our only hope is in God's ways, through which forgiveness and responsibility come in balance. There is indeed another bridge, one on which a body was broken so that a path was made that we might cross over and live. In that cross lie both judgment and mercy. The Judge of all the earth cannot be fooled by shades of meaning, nor was Christ obliterated by the shadows of death.

Thanks be to God, the Father of our Lord Jesus Christ, who is our help and hope in ages past and years to come.

REFLECTION QUESTIONS

1. "At the heart of the law is God's very character. . . . There is a spiritual essence that precedes moral injunctions." Explain how this is true.
2. What does the parable of the prodigal son and his father reveal about the heart of God?

PERSONAL APPLICATION

1. If your life were cast in the pages of Scripture, what character most resembles you apart from Christ's forgiveness—the questioning Pharisee, fearful adulterous woman, prodigal son, or angry brother?
2. Where do you need Christ's rescue today?

43

SCANDAL OF THE CROSS

Jews demand signs and Greeks look for
wisdom, but we preach Christ crucified: a
stumbling block to Jews and foolishness
to Gentiles, but to those whom God has
called, both Jews and Greeks, Christ the
power of God and the wisdom of God.
For the foolishness of God is wiser than
human wisdom, and the weakness of
God is stronger than human strength.

1 CORINTHIANS 1:22-25

What a striking verse in the New Testament in which the apostle Paul refers to the cross of Jesus Christ as foolishness to the Greek and a stumbling block to the Jew. One can readily understand why he would say that. After all, to the Greek mind, sophistication, philosophy, and learning were exalted pursuits. How could One crucified possibly spell knowledge?

To the Jewish mind, on the other hand, there was a cry and a longing to be free. In their history, they had been attacked by numerous powers and often humiliated by occupying forces. Whether it was by the Assyrians or the Babylonians or the Romans, Jerusalem had been repeatedly plundered and its people left homeless. What would the Hebrews have wanted more than someone who could take up their cause and altogether repel the enemy? How could a Messiah who was crucified possibly be of any help?

To the Greek, the cross was foolishness. To the Jew, it was a stumbling block. What is it about the cross of Christ that so roundly defies everything that power relishes? Crucifixion was humiliating and excruciatingly painful, so much so that the Romans who specialized in the art of torture assured their own citizenry that a Roman could never be crucified.

May I add that for this among other reasons, our Muslim friends consider the cross a sign of weakness and hence bearing no resemblance to power.[1] "How can the God of all creation be so humiliated?" a Muslim questioner once asked me. Yet, when the Mel Gibson film

The Passion of the Christ was shown in the United Arab Emirates to packed audiences, many would walk out wiping away tears and saying, "We had no idea how He had been treated."

Should that not give us pause? Think of it: humiliation and agony. To what end? Why such barbarism? This was the path Jesus chose with which to reach out for you and for me.

You see, this thing we call *sin*, but which we so tragically minimize, breaks the grandeur for which we were created. It brings indignity to our essence and pain to our existence. It separates us from God. Someone has rightly said that the worst effect of sin is shown, not in suffering or in bodily defacement, but rather in "the discrowned faculties, the unworthy loves, the low ideals, the brutalized and the enslaved spirit."[2]

Think of that, phrase by phrase:

Discrowned faculties: all the brilliance and creative genius we have within humanity, and yet we stoop to such base pursuits.

Unworthy loves: practices we ought to despise, yet we stoop to such depraved pursuits (pornography, violence, hate, profanity).

Low ideals: we ought to set our vision for things that are noble, yet we spend time and effort on the ignoble.

The brutalized and enslaved spirit: We sink deeper and deeper into bad habits till we enslave ourselves. This is the worst form of slavery of which we so seldom speak.

On the way to the cross two thousand years ago, Jesus took the ultimate indignity, the ultimate debasement, the ultimate penalty, and the ultimate pain to bring us back to the dignity of a relationship with God and the healing of our souls. Will you remember that this was done for you and receive His gift?

You will then discover that it is sin that is foolishness, not the provision. Our greatest weakness is not an enemy from without but one from within. Our own weak wills cause us to stumble. But Jesus Christ frees us from the foolishness of sin and the weakness of our selves.

This is the very reason the apostle Paul went on to say that he preached Jesus Christ as one crucified, which was both the power of God and the wisdom of God. This is not scandalous. What is scandalous is that we do not see our own folly and failure. This is the wisdom of God correcting our folly and the grace of God overcoming our egos. This is the love of God overriding our hate.

Come to the cross in these days given for our contemplation and find out His power and His wisdom. Paul was won by the resurrection, but he made an understanding of the cross his pursuit. He was of Jewish stock and the product of Greek learning. He realized all of that was nothing when he understood how the cross was the profound answer to our foolish ways of thinking and living. Next time you see a cross, remember it is God's wisdom for our failures.

REFLECTION QUESTIONS

1. Why do Muslims consider the cross of Christ so offensive? (To dig deeper, see colleague Abdu Murray's article referenced on page 300.)
2. How are God's glory, power, love, and justice displayed at the cross?

PERSONAL APPLICATION

1. Take time to consider one or all of the phrases listed on page 237 (e.g. "unworthy loves"). Ask your heavenly Father to fill you with the fullness of His Spirit and to help you surrender to His correction and grace.
2. Thank God that He frees us from the foolishness of sin and the weakness of ourselves. How might you also be an example of His kindness and mercy this week?

44

IMAGINATION AND THE WILL

Although they knew God, they neither
glorified him as God nor gave thanks to him,
but their thinking became futile and their
foolish hearts were darkened. Although they
claimed to be wise, they became fools and
exchanged the glory of the immortal God
for images made to look like a mortal human
being and birds and animals and reptiles.

ROMANS 1:21–23

When our son, Nathan, was only nine years old, he decided he was going to write a book. He did this because he saw me at the computer every day and thought writing would be fun. He did quite a job actually, featuring a murder, a kidnapping, and all the other horrible stuff that grabs a person's attention. There was some such tragedy or atrocity on every page. He would devotedly sit down and start writing away. It was fascinating to watch his intensity in crafting a story.

But one day I noticed that he was sitting at the dining table, pen in hand, the story in front of him, and tears running down his face. I wondered what on earth had happened. I never for a moment imagined what his answer would be when I went to his side. I put my arm around him and said, "What's the matter, son?"

He kept wiping the tears and said, "I just know the dog is going to die."

"What dog?" I asked.

He named the dog that he had introduced in that story. I did everything I could to keep a straight face as he unfolded the story line, which involved this marvelous little dog that now took ill. He just knew that death would be the logical end to the impressive pet.

Isn't that something? The power of the imagination even to draw in the storyteller and become sovereign over the one creating the fantasy in the first place! Reality had its long reach even in the world of one's own creation. Nathan could stay with the fantastic only so long. He had to get to the fantastically true.

I have often looked back upon my own life, and even as I have listened to others, I have come to realize how powerful the imagination is and how it can be used for good or evil. I believe it was the French thinker Pascal who said: "Put the world's greatest philosopher on a plank that is wider than need be; if there is a precipice below, although his reason may convince him that he is safe, his imagination will prevail."[1]

In other words, the imagination can even distort reality. This is why God gives us the imagination to dream but the intuition, conscience, and reason to govern such aspirations with caution. Even the laws of aerodynamics can show us how to soar, but we cannot violate those laws. Imagination is a good thing, but it cannot violate the boundaries that govern reality.

This is just one of the reasons I believe the Lord Jesus tells us to keep our eye single, meaning having the moral vision to discern good from evil (Matthew 6:22). What we see and what we enjoy in our seeing has a direct bearing upon the imagination. By the way, those in the movie industry who deal in the world of fantasy would do well to remember this. Just because the movie can create a fantasy does not mean it should do so. I remember a music director telling me how he chose to craft his music when the scene was debased. He would put in the sounds of horror, just to introduce caution to any who would chase such wild fantasies.

Let me ask you this question: Are you disciplined to bring the reason and will to bear upon the imagination?

As I write this, I have just left the rather relatively unspoiled terrain of Nepal. In a strange way, in spite of the mix of plenty and want, it's a very pretty country. On a clear day, you can see the majestic protrusions from the Himalayas, and of course, the crown jewel of peaks, Mount Everest. The smiling Sherpas may point to their methods and the skyline may point upwards, but if you were to climb even the mountain that is not for all humanity to scale, you would see bodies along the way of those who did not heed the warning signs to turn around and head back. The price paid for such violations has been heavy.

The apostle Paul, in his letter to the church at Rome, chronicles how the human mind works when it turns away from God and His warning signs to us. He says that although people knew God, they did not respond to that which they knew and as a result their imagination became corrupt. Knowledge of truth and the response to it are the surest strengths against the power of the imagination. May yours be that strength today to keep the imagination in check.

REFLECTION QUESTIONS

1. Can you think of ways imagination has been used for both good and evil, whether in a fictional work or an actual event?
2. How do reason and will bear upon the imagination?

PERSONAL APPLICATION

1. Jesus tells us to keep our eye single. How might His gracious admonition guard your steps today?
2. Our imaginations can distort reality and disregard the boundaries God set for our protection. Or perhaps you've stifled the good gift of imagination. Ask God to heal and renew your imagination so that you can receive "every good and perfect gift . . . from the Father" (James 1:17).

45

COPING WITH LIFE'S TURBULENCE

We continually ask God to fill you with the knowledge of his will through all the wisdom and understanding that the Spirit gives, so that you may live a life worthy of the Lord and please him in every way: bearing fruit in every good work, growing in the knowledge of God, being strengthened with all power according to his glorious might so that you may have great endurance and patience.

COLOSSIANS 1:9–11

There is a story told about onetime heavyweight boxing champion Muhammad Ali. Ali was flying to one of his engagements and during the flight, the aircraft ran into foul weather. Moderate turbulence began to toss the plane about. Of course, all nervous fliers well know that when a pilot signals "moderate turbulence," he or she is implying, *If you have any religious beliefs, it is time to start expressing them.*

The passengers were instructed to fasten their seat belts immediately, and all complied but Ali. So the flight attendant approached him and requested that he observe the captain's order, only to hear Ali audaciously respond, "Superman don't need no seat belt." The flight attendant, however, did not miss a beat but quickly fired in reply, "Superman don't need no airplane either!"

Recently, another humorous story made the rounds about two of the most prominent football (soccer) players of our time: Cristiano Ronaldo and Lionel Messi. Somebody joked that Ronaldo made the comment that God had sent him into the world to show the world how to play football. A reporter told that story to Messi and asked, "What do you think of that?" Messi paused and said, "Honestly, I don't remember sending him."

Anyone who knows Messi would doubt that he would say anything like that. But it made for a great story. Humor aside, that's the way that often those in highly competitive sports see themselves. The best this, the greatest that, or the finest ever.

I draw attention to those stories because I would like to consider the larger context in which many of us find ourselves. Some of us will be granted access to the best education, others offered an array of possibilities for achievement. Many of us work diligently to position ourselves for extraordinary success in a rapidly changing world. In any of these possible triumphs, a sense of invincibility can be engendered—regardless of what measure of turbulence may lie ahead.

Yet unfortunately, academic or material advancement does not necessarily confer wisdom. As someone rightly quipped, "It may be a smartphone, but it is not a wise phone." How foolish it would be for us to take what generations preceding us have valued in coping with life's turbulence and cast it all aside because we are *modern*. Now of course even *modern* is not good enough; we are *postmodern*. We sound more and more like a product—*super ultra*, *ultra plus*, and so on. In the process of so-called advances, we unwittingly forget what is needed to preserve any gain. Those values are cast in stone.

As G. K. Chesterton aptly advised his generation, before pulling any fence down, we should always pause long enough to find out why it was put there in the first place.[1] Removing ancient markers or boundaries is a risky endeavor. It is a valuable day in life when we realize that laws are in place not just for another's benefit but for ours as well.

As I see our world, I see a terrifying reality. Governments seem to falter along two extremes. There are demagogues who think they alone matter. There are so called democracies where people think freedom alone matters. Both commit the blunder of forgetting there is a law above our laws. There are values by which we must be governed.

In other words, we need wisdom as we process and distill all knowledge. But where does one find it? The irony of the call to wisdom in the Bible is that the one who spoke most about it kept it all in the realm of writing great one-liners but did not apply that wisdom in living. This is a painful reminder that knowing does not guarantee doing. Doing engages the will and a preset commitment.

In one of his proverbs, King Solomon wrote,

> Blessed are those who find wisdom,
>> those who gain understanding,
> for she is more profitable than silver
>> and yields better returns than gold.
> She is more precious than rubies;
>> nothing you desire can compare with her. (Proverbs 3:13–15)

By this same king we are told, "The fear of the LORD is the beginning of wisdom" (Proverbs 9:10; Psalm 111:10).

In other words, reverence for God is where wisdom starts, with a recognition that there is a Giver of knowledge and wisdom. We begin with reverence for our Creator and translate that into reverence for His creation and His call upon our lives.

On days when we are tempted by thoughts of invincibility, might we remember that falsely posing as a superman will only ensure a crash landing. There's "kryptonite" at every turn in places where we are overwhelmed by turbulent forces and weakening attacks upon inner strength. We can reach our potential strength only when we know who is all-powerful and humbly bow before Him. I pray we will humbly seek wisdom and follow it to its Source so that He will lift us to glorious heights, for His honor and our purpose.

REFLECTION QUESTIONS

1. What does it mean to say there is a law above our laws—and what is this law?
2. How do both social media and our sports-obsessed world encourage us to project ourselves as invincible? What are the risks in doing so?

PERSONAL APPLICATION

1. Knowing does not guarantee doing. Doing engages the will and a preset commitment. Ask God to direct your steps to do what He has set before you this week.
2. Can you recall when you have been "wise in your own eyes" (Proverbs 3:7) and the results that ensued? Pray through the entire prayer in Colossians 1:9–14 and "ask God to fill you with the knowledge of his will through all the wisdom and understanding that the Spirit gives" (v. 9).

46

IS IT WORTH IT?

Jesus declared, "I am the bread of life. Whoever comes to me will never go hungry, and whoever believes in me will never be thirsty. But as I told you, you have seen me and still you do not believe. All those the Father gives me will come to me, and whoever comes to me I will never drive away. For I have come down from heaven not to do my will but to do the will of him who sent me."

JOHN 6:35–38

Despite all denials of truth as a category, people still hunger for it. The real question that haunts us is not whether truth exists, but whether it is worth it, and then the toughest question of all: Where can I find it?

On August 6, 1961, a twenty-six-year-old Soviet cosmonaut named Gherman Titov became the second Soviet to orbit the earth and return safely. Sometime later he recounted his experience while speaking at the Century 21 Exposition in Seattle. Titov declared that on his excursion into space, he looked for God but didn't find Him. The Soviet's entire political and economic theory being based on an atheistic framework made his affirmation a justification for their foundational belief.

Someone humorously quipped, "Had he stepped out of his spacecraft, he certainly would have." Titov, of course, had moved beyond the discipline of technological gain to draw theological blood. A man who never in a million years would have believed that his spaceship was an accidental collection of atoms somehow believed that the universe itself was such an accident. One great step for science became an immensely greater leap in philosophy.

Years later on Christmas Day, 1968, three American astronauts were the first human beings to go around the "dark" side of the moon. Captured by the awe of the universe, the astronauts echoed the only words that seemed fitting. Those words were from the first line of the Bible: "In the beginning God created the heaven and the earth . . ." (KJV).

Two similar experiences of awe and splendor yielded two diametrically opposed conclusions. These two incidents carried off into space the most debated question on earth: *Does God exist?*

The answer to that question has a greater bearing on your life than anything else does. Personal and national destinies are inextricably bound to this issue. Our entire human frame of moral reference is determined by whether or not God exists. Our purpose in life is determined by that, whether we are here by design or by no agency whatsoever and just by chance. Who we are and why we exist logically flows from the question of God's existence.

In the 1950s, Encyclopedia Britannica, Inc. published a multiple-volume set titled *The Great Books of the Western World*. It is a treasure-house of great Western thinkers from Socrates to Aquinas to Pascal. A storehouse of information. One of the main editors was a man by the name of Mortimer Adler. In an interview years ago, Professor Adler was asked why, of all the themes covered in *The Great Books*, was the longest essay on God?

Adler replied without any hesitation that it was because more consequences for our lives follow from that one issue than any other issue.

It is the most logical answer to have been given. One's belief in values of any kind follows from one's belief or disbelief in God.

It was Mahatma Gandhi who said, "God is truth."[1] If he meant by that statement that truth as an idea is God, then I would take issue with it. But if he meant that everything that the notion of truth represents is in the very person of God, then I would grant that premise. In other words, truth matters because God matters. God matters comprehensively, and therefore truth matters.

The question, therefore, is not whether the pursuit of truth is worth it or not, for it is the only thing that is ultimately worthwhile, so valuable that it has often been blockaded by a bodyguard of lies.

But we might ask, "What's wrong with a lie?"

I might safely add one word: "Everything."

For one, we would think it is morally wrong, would we not? We would not excuse it by saying, "Oh well, people have different views." Does it matter that morality has to be rightly understood, unless this is a moral universe? And how can this be a moral universe unless it is created by God? Personhood has no intrinsic worth apart from the person of God being the First Cause. The intelligibility in this universe and the immense capacity of the moral law point us to a transcendent order set in place by God.

What is more, we don't have to go into outer space to find Him. He comes to us in our inner space, the inner space of our lives. Jesus said, "The one who comes to Me I will by no means cast out" (John 6:37 NKJV).

The truth we seek is revealed in the person of Jesus Christ, and His answers conform to reality rightly understood. In knowing Him, you find truth and life. When that inner space is conquered, outer space confirms what God has revealed in His Word and in nature. That is why the pursuit of truth is worth it—because it seeks to know the mind of God.

REFLECTION QUESTIONS

1. What question has a greater bearing on your life than anything else? Why?
2. What points to a transcendent order set in place by God? Explain.

PERSONAL APPLICATION

1. One's belief in values of any kind follows from one's belief or disbelief in God. Take an inventory of your values (e.g., charity, honesty) and consider how they flow from or perhaps contradict your perspective of God.
2. What does the "inner space" of your life look like? Is it in turmoil, constant motion, at peace? Ask Jesus to feed you with His bread of life and fill your soul with His abundance and peace.

47

ARE YOU LONELY?

The Lord confides in those who fear him;
he makes his covenant known to them.
My eyes are ever on the Lord,
for only he will release my feet from the snare.
Turn to me and be gracious to me,
for I am lonely and afflicted.
Relieve the troubles of my heart
and free me from my anguish.

PSALM 25:14–17

Elvis Presley once sang "Are You Lonesome Tonight?" Although he was not exactly a philosopher, and his question was more in the romantic tones of an evening together, I think he spoke of a deep hunger in the human heart.

Writer Thomas Wolfe, having himself lived an emotionally turbulent life, articulated one of the deepest aches within the human heart. Consider his words; I believe they are profound:

> The whole conviction of my life now rests upon the belief that loneliness, far from being a rare and curious phenomenon, peculiar to myself and to a few other solitary people, is the central and inevitable feature of human existence. . . . All this hideous doubt, despair and dark confusion of the soul a lonely man must know, for he is united to no image save that which he creates himself. He is bolstered by no other knowledge save that which he can gather for himself with the vision of his own eyes and brain. He is sustained and cheered and aided by no party. He is given comfort by no creed. He has no faith in him except his own, and often that faith deserts him, leaving him shaken and filled with impotence. Then it seems to him that his life has come to nothing. That he is ruined, lost, and broken, past redemption, and that morning, that bright and shining morning with its promise of new beginnings, will never come upon the earth again as it did once.[1]

Has this author exposed a throbbing nerve of a reality that holds us all in its grip? Is he telling it like it is?

Tempting though it might be for the optimist to dismiss these words as cynically conceived in some dark moment of despair, there are many who would echo the same feeling of desolation. In fact, I would venture to say that this cry of loneliness is felt by all, though better suppressed by some. As one actress recently quipped, "We are all in this together alone."

Herein lies the malady. It is a torn self in search of being put back together. That's why I believe the answer is to be found in the only pursuit that pulls our lives together into a focused expression. Worship in spirit and in truth is what captures this coalescing within. Worship alone brings all expressions into one purpose. And as we fear (revere) the Lord, He offers us intimacy: "The friendship of the LORD is for those who fear him, and he makes known to them his covenant" (Psalm 25:14 ESV). What an amazing truth!

The problem of loneliness is indeed universal. The hymn-writer who penned the beloved Christmas carol "O Little Town of Bethlehem" captured this idea well in the words, "The hopes and fears of all the years are met in thee tonight."[2]

At the risk of sounding trite, may I ask you: Are you lonely this day? Do you sense time and again that you are mangled within? Are your hopes and fears pinned on the future hope of some companion or accomplishment to bring you solace? Or have you brought them to the One who alone can bring you lasting hope and a future?

May I suggest that you bring your lonely heart to God and allow Him to do His work in your life by putting you back together, in your affections and your pursuits? It's not good enough to bring God your heart for a night. It has to be done daily for life itself.

REFLECTION QUESTIONS

1. What is the one pursuit that pulls our lives together, and how does it begin to answer the problem of loneliness?
2. What is "the friendship of the LORD"? Spend time in Psalm 25 or John 15 to pursue this truth in Scripture.

PERSONAL APPLICATION

1. When do you most feel lonely—and how do you attempt to meet this need? When do you most feel loved?
2. Ask God to encourage you with the knowledge of His friendship. How might this amazing truth direct your path today and open a door of ministry to someone else?

48

FINDING THE PERFECT GIFT

Don't be deceived, my dear brothers and
sisters. Every good and perfect gift is from
above, coming down from the Father of the
heavenly lights, who does not change like
shifting shadows. He chose to give us birth
through the word of truth, that we might
be a kind of firstfruits of all he created.

JAMES 1:16–18

sn't it ironic that the more we have access to, the further we are from finding the answer to our struggle for an overarching purpose for life? We are like the little boy surrounded by Christmas gifts. Minutes after the gifts have been torn into, the poor child sits staring at the wall, saddened at having exhausted so much in so little time.

Likewise, having tasted of every new experience that has come along, we too wonder like children on Christmas morning where all the promised fulfillment has gone. Most of the excitement seems to be in the anticipation and expectation rather than in the procurement or the unwrapping.

Our world has seen many advances that offer the promise of a new day. First, we live in the age of communication. Never before have we had such means to transmit content or create desire. Yet even with such capacities, the walls between races, cultures, and generations still stand. Years ago people were saying that television and communication were going to make this world a more peaceful planet and the United Nations was going to be the answer for our utopia. We now have media of every kind, once only a pipe dream, and yet the world always seems to be on edge.

Second, we live in the age of technology. But it has delivered a bill of goods for which the cost exacted is the loss of peace of mind. Each new invention was supposed to save us time. Yet less time is spent in building relationships while more is invested in the trappings of our "conveniences." At the end of the day it is more likely that family members are sitting with their own cell phones than they are willing to sit and enjoy a conversation around a meal together. It's a sad loss.

Third, medicine has vastly improved our lives, and yet we have lost the definition of life itself. How we have changed! "For the wise men of old," said C. S. Lewis, "the cardinal problem has been how to conform the soul to reality, and the solution had been knowledge, self-discipline, and virtue. For magic and applied science alike, the problem is how to subdue reality to the wishes of men."[1] Some change, isn't it? If living is at the mercy of the moment, then dying is as much an option as living.

Fourth, human sexuality has never been more studied and pandered to in public, yet we have never been more confused about what is right and good. Young minds are exposed to sights and sounds that foster cravings that no human experience can match or placate. Sadly, what is worse, the built-in mystery and gift of sexual enjoyment has moved from the marital relationship to any opportune moment for gratification. We are more indulgent than ever and more unfulfilled than ever.

These advances have not been able to soothe the cry for meaning heard from millions of hearts, have they? *Why am I here? What is life all about? Am I just to find a way to tranquilize my boredom?* On one day we walk to and fro. On another day we walk fro and to.

If the answer does not lie in gadgets and toys and entertainment, where can we go? What button can we press to win meaning and fulfillment?

The Bible says, "Every good and perfect gift is from above, coming down from the Father of the heavenly lights, who does not change like shifting shadows." Just look at the Giver and then the promise. The Giver is God Himself, who gives as a loving Father. Remember the parent who gave you your first bike or your first watch? I remember both occasions. With the watch, I walked around as if my arm were in a sling: I looked constantly at it. I was in my mid-teens when that watch was given. Watches were not easy to get in India. The imported brands were what was preferred. My mom had asked a neighbor who was a pilot within the land to ask his brother, who flew internationally, to please bring me a watch. On the day it arrived I remember thanking my parents profusely for caring enough to get me that watch. My parents made it possible.

The God of the Scriptures is the Giver of life itself. What a gift to be enjoyed. What a treasure to guard! It's more than the gift of life. It is the gift of His presence in salvation. More specifically, His presence is our consolation. His mercy gives us our salvation. His glory extends immeasurably beyond all of our faltering answers and fleeting solutions, and yet, His love is extended to each of us personally.

Let us not be like the little boy surrounded by gifts but not knowing joy. Go to the Giver, who alone gives us perpetual wonder and fulfillment. His generous heart fills our needy hearts.

REFLECTION QUESTIONS

1. How have communication and technology changed the way we relate to each other? Have they brought more intimacy and connection or less? How?
2. Why is the enjoyment of a gift often so fleeting? Can you think of a gift that's brought you lasting joy or still touches your heart? Why is that?

PERSONAL APPLICATION

1. How might you guard the treasure of God's gift—His very presence and consolation—this week?
2. Consider how your view of God's generosity or lack thereof informs the way you go to Him in prayer and relate to others. Ask God to conform your view of Him to who He really is.

49

SAFELY INTO THE UNKNOWN

I have kept my feet from every evil path
so that I might obey your word.
I have not departed from your laws,
for you yourself have taught me.
How sweet are your words to my taste,
sweeter than honey to my mouth!
I gain understanding from your precepts;
therefore I hate every wrong path.
Your word is a lamp for my feet,
a light on my path.

PSALM 119:101–105

One of the most beautiful moments in the book *The Pilgrim's Progress* is when Pilgrim arrives at the hill called Calvary. He has been carrying his burden of sin in his journey. (I have shared a portion of this story previously, but I think it bears repeating.) An amazing thing happens as Pilgrim reaches the cross of Calvary. The first is the falling off of the weight of sin. Then he is greeted by the three Shining Ones: the angel of dawn, the angel of daybreak, and the angel of dusk.

The first angel says, "Son, thy sins be forgiven thee" and puts a mark on his forehead. The second one replaces Pilgrim's tattered clothes with a new robe and sandals. The third angel hands him a scroll—the map toward the Celestial Gate. It's an amazing threefold action. The old life is traded for the new inheritance, and hence the mark on the forehead. The second gift is the new covering as a child of God. The third is the guide on how to walk the rest of the journey till Pilgrim reaches his final stopping point at the end of life.

The guide for life presupposes whom you belong to. That is the first prerequisite, to know that you are not your own; you are a child of God as you come to the cross. That is where you die to self and live for Him. That is the true intersection where the crossroads of life meet.

I remember a man from Pakistan telling me how he attended an Easter church service once and was terribly bored by the speaker—until the speaker reached the end and made these two statements:

> In dying you live.
> In surrendering, you win.

Those statements reversed everything in the way he thought. Dying to self and personal glory is the starting point to really living. Augustine said it best: "You have made us for yourself and our hearts are restless until they find their rest in thee."[1]

The next step suggested by the gift of new clothes to Pilgrim is the change that life brings. It's not enough to lay claim to be God's child. We must live that life and wear His coat well.

Finally, the map for life is given. That is the key to growth and maturity: how to handle disappointment. How to handle failure. How to interpret success. How to live for that which is eternal.

The question is how and where do we find that map? God has given us four resources. First is His Word given to us in the Holy Scriptures. Your life should begin each day with that Word. The psalmist says, "Your word is a lamp for my feet, a light on my path" (Psalm 119:105).

The second is His indwelling presence, which God promises to us. As you talk to Him, He speaks to you and guides with His still, small voice.

The third is to have a life of accountability. Those who love you must have the courage to correct you when they see you are on the wrong path.

Fourth, God will bring circumstances into your life to help you grow. These are not always delightful. Sometimes they are painful.

In 1939 King George VI spoke to the world at a very troubled time. He quoted this poem in his Christmas Day message:

I said to the man who stood at the gate of the year:
"Give me a light that I may tread safely into the unknown."
And he replied:
"Go out into the darkness and put your hand into the Hand
    of God.
That shall be to you better than light and safer than a known way."[2]

Through His Word, you put your hand into His hand, and He will guide you safely into the unknown.

REFLECTION QUESTIONS

1. Think about the two brief statements that changed the direction of the Pakistani man's life. Where do you find the ideas of dying to self and living for God in Scripture?
2. What four resources has God given to guide us?

PERSONAL APPLICATION

1. "The guide for life presupposes whom you belong to." Are you being directed by God as His child, or are other influences pulling you onto a divergent path? How do you know when God is guiding you?
2. Have you learned to handle disappointment? How about failure and success? How might you grow in one of these areas this week?

50

PEACE LIKE A RIVER

You will keep in perfect peace
those whose minds are steadfast,
because they trust in you.
Trust in the LORD forever,
for the LORD, the LORD himself, is the Rock eternal.

ISAIAH 26:3–4

There is a story told of an American soldier hiding in a bunker during the Korean War. When his commander ordered him to rescue some of his fallen mates on the front lines, the soldier nodded his head, took a covert glance at his watch, stalled till his commanding officer was out of sight, and simply made no move. Several minutes went by, and a colleague reminded him of his rescue assignment. Again, he looked at his watch and delayed. Finally, he leaped out of the bunker and fearlessly began carrying his compatriots to safety.

At the end of the day, a friend asked him to explain his curious actions. The soldier said, "I was afraid because I knew I was not ready to die. I was waiting until my fear would be overcome by the assurance of something greater. At a certain time every hour my mother promised that she would pray for me. Remembering this as I looked out from the bunker, I knew that no matter what awaited me, I could face it."

Over the years, I have since talked to scores of people in many lands. Everyone tells you his or her own story, and invariably it would involve a friend or a family who played a role in bringing the person to that point. No one gets to where they are without the prayers and the efforts of someone else. It was Andrew for Peter, Ananias for Paul, the mother and grandmother for Timothy—and the list goes on. The goal of all these efforts was to help someone make peace with God and stay in God's peace. It is not a momentary thing. It is a daily walk.

There is no doubt in my mind that when I first found my relationship with Jesus, the peace was overwhelming. But I am equally certain how that stability is threatened, and each day one needs to make sure that peace is not shattered by a careless choice or decision.

Indeed, the Bible says it so well with a succinct promise in the book of Isaiah: "You will keep in perfect peace those whose minds are steadfast, because they trust in you" (Isaiah 26:3). In fact, when I first heard this story of the Korean War soldier, my mind wandered back to when I was in Vietnam speaking at a service attended by several American airmen. They were in full uniform, many alert for missions that would claim their lives. I will never forget how the closing hymn resounded throughout the room as their voices sang from the depths of the emotions that welled up from within them:

> When peace, like a river, attendeth my way,
> When sorrows like sea billows roll,
> Whatever my lot, Thou hast taught me to say,
> It is well, it is well with my soul![1]

But let us also not miss the foundational reason for this peace, stated by the songwriter in the third stanza:

> My sin—oh, the bliss of this glorious tho't,
> My sin—not in part, but the whole—
> Is nailed to the cross and I bear it no more
> Praise the Lord, Praise the Lord, O my soul![2]

I had already by that point spent several months in the region, and I had begun to sense how many had gone into action but never returned. So their uncertainty was with reason. What they needed more than anything else was peace within for a greater reason.

You see, it was Thomas Merton who observed that man is not at peace with his fellow man because he is not at peace with himself, and he is not at peace with himself because he is not at peace with God.[3] Even as the apostle Paul said, "Since we have been justified through faith, we have peace with God through our Lord Jesus Christ, through whom we have gained access by faith into this grace in which we now stand" (Romans 5:1–2).

So what lies beneath our struggle is a daily routine based on a momentous decision. That decision is to deal with what we do to hurt ourselves, not what others do to hurt us. The attacks of others simply will not succeed if we have taken the protection to guard our souls. That was the admonition to Timothy from Paul: "Be on your guard" and "Guard the good deposit that was entrusted to you" (2 Timothy 4:15; 1:14). Have you ever been threatened by anyone? When you post a guard at the door, you sleep peacefully because someone else is awake for you. The best guardian of your own peace is the precaution you take to keep your heart guarded for God and by God.

Dear friend, may you know today that the freedom to have peace without begins with the freedom from evil within, and may you stand on this foundational reason for peace. In other words, it is a condition of the soul.

REFLECTION QUESTIONS

1. According to the hymn writer and Scripture, what is the foundational reason for a Christian's peace?
2. What is the "momentous decision" we make daily whether we realize it or not? How does this decision relate to the apostle Paul's admonition to Timothy?

PERSONAL APPLICATION

1. To get where you are today, you needed the prayers and the efforts of someone else. Who has prayed for you over the years or been a support and an ally? Take time today to thank that person and God. Likewise, whom are you praying for faithfully?
2. What are you doing today to help you rest securely in God's peace and to guard the good deposit of His Spirit entrusted to you?

51

WHERE GOD WAS HOMELESS

"Come, you who are blessed by my
Father; take your inheritance, the kingdom
prepared for you since the creation of
the world. For I was hungry and you gave
me something to eat, I was thirsty and
you gave me something to drink, I was
a stranger and you invited me in. . . .
"Truly I tell you, whatever you did for
one of the least of these brothers and
sisters of mine, you did for me."

MATTHEW 25:34–35, 40

Some years ago we were spending Christmas in the home of my wife's parents. It was not a happy time in the household. Much had gone wrong during the preceding weeks, and a weight of sadness hung over the home. Yet, in the midst of all that, my mother-in-law kept her routine habit of asking people who would likely have no place to go to share Christmas dinner with us.

That year she invited a man who was, by everyone's estimate, somewhat of an odd person, quite eccentric in his demeanor. Not much was known about him at the church except that he came regularly, sat alone, and left without much conversation. He obviously lived alone and was quite a sad-looking, solitary figure. He was our Christmas guest.

Because of other happenings in the house (including one daughter being taken to the hospital for the birth of her first child), everything was in confusion. All of our emotions were on edge. It fell upon me, in turn, to entertain this gentleman. I must confess that I did not appreciate it. Owing to a heavy life of travel year-round, I have jealously guarded my Christmases as time to be with my family. This was not going to be such a privilege, and I was not happy. As I sat in the living room, entertaining him while others were busy, I thought to myself, *This is going to be one of the most miserable Christmases of my life.*

Somehow we got through the evening. He evidently loved the meal, the fire crackling in the background, the snow outside, the Christmas carols playing, and a rather weighty theological discussion in which he and I engaged—at his instigation, I might add. He was a very well-read man and, as I found out, loved to grapple with heavy theological themes. I do too, but frankly, not during an evening that has been set aside to enjoy life's quiet moments.

At the end of the night when he bade us all good-bye, he reached out and took the hand of each of us, one by one, and said, "Thank you for the best Christmas of my life. I will never forget it." He walked out into the dark, snowy night, back into his solitary existence.

My heart sank in self-indictment at those tender words. I had to draw on every nerve in my being to keep from breaking down with tears. Just a few short years later, relatively young, and therefore to our surprise, he passed away. I have relived that Christmas many times in my memory. That year God taught me a lesson. A home can reflect and distribute the love of Christ.

The first time I walked through the noisy streets of Bethlehem and endured its smells, I gained a whole new sense of the difference between our Christmas carols, glamorizing the sweetness of the "little town of Bethlehem," and the harsh reality of God becoming flesh and making a home among us. Jesus' earthly address changes our own. Christ comes at Christmas—and each and every day—to show us what it means to live.

REFLECTION QUESTIONS

1. Consider how Jesus's words in Matthew 25 disrupt us with His call to surrender.
2. Read Luke 2:1–20. What does the first Christmas story reveal about God's invitation and the significance of hospitality?

PERSONAL APPLICATION

1. Do you recall a similar Christmas or time when you were interrupted? How might you open your heart today to those God has placed in your life?
2. Perhaps you are like the lonely man in this story. Ask your heavenly Father where you might find community and be a blessing to someone else.

52

GIVING ALL

"A son honors his father, and a slave his
master. If I am a father, where is the honor
due me? If I am a master, where is the respect
due me?" says the LORD Almighty. . . .
"When you offer blind animals for sacrifice,
is that not wrong? When you sacrifice lame
or diseased animals, is that not wrong?
Try offering them to your governor!
Would he be pleased with you? Would he
accept you?" says the LORD Almighty.

MALACHI 1:6, 8

When I was about twelve or thirteen years old, I was asked by our Sunday school teacher if I would be willing to play Joseph in the Nativity mime. I was on the verge of saying no to this request, for most of the Christmas story was hidden under the weight of ceremony for me, and I really did not know what all that meant. But then I was told what I would need to do. Basically, I would walk Mary to the altar with her arm in mine, stand there, turn around, have her put her arm in mine, and then walk out. No words, no theological insight, no big acting skill needed. When I met who was going to play Mary, I decided this would be quite a thrill.

I arrived at the church early and was walking around with time to kill. At the altar, I happened upon a silver bowl with wafers in it on a table. Having very little knowledge of what this could be, I took a handful of those wafers and enjoyed them as I admired all the great art and statuary in that fine cathedral. Suddenly I saw the vicar coming out of the vestry and walking straight toward me. I politely greeted him and continued my enjoyment of the biscuits in hand. He stopped, stared, and quite out of control, shouted, "What are you doing?"

As surprised by his outburst as he was at my activity, I said, "I am Joseph in the Nativity mime."

That evidently was not what he was asking. "What is that in your hand?" he demanded.

As he stared me down from head to toe, he could see that there were more in my pocket. I received the most incomprehensible tongue-lashing to which I had ever been subjected. The word that he kept repeating was the word "sacrilege." I didn't want to check out its meaning, for I was sure this was the end of the line for me, having done something I did not even know how to pronounce.

Years later, I could not help but be reminded of this incident when I was reading G. Campbell Morgan's definition of *sacrilege*. He said that it is normally defined as taking something that belongs to God and using it profanely. You may recall the instance in the book of Daniel when Belshazzar took the vessels in the temple and used them for his night of carousing and blasphemy. That was a sacrilegious use. The same applies to our bodies that are intended to be "vessels" in God's service, or "temples" as the inner sanctuary of worship. When we put the body to profane use, we are committing a sacrilege.

But sacrilege, said Morgan, does not consist only of such profane use. In its worst form, it consists of taking something and giving it to God when it means absolutely nothing to you.[1] Giving God the "left-overs" of your life rather than the firstfruits. That was the charge God brought against His people when He said, "You bring the lame and the blind and the sick as an offering, is this not evil?"

In contrast, giving all that is your best to God is worship at its core. This cannot be done without the sacrifice of the acclaim and adulation of the world.

If we were to pause for only a few moments and take stock, we would see how close we all come to sacrilege each day. Do we give God the best of our time? Do we give God the best of our energies?

Do we give God the best of our thinking? Do we give God the best of our wealth? Do we give God the best of our dreams and plans? Or does the world get our best and God merely gets the leftovers?

As the year closes and a new one approaches, may we remember the One who came among us, taught us His mission, and then sent the Spirit to guide us in it. Might our lives echo the heartfelt words of Charles Wesley:

> O Thou who camest from above
> The fire celestial to impart,
> Kindle a flame of sacred love
> On the mean altar of my heart!
>
> There let it for Thy glory burn
> With inextinguishable blaze,
> And trembling to its source return
> In humble prayer and fervent praise.
>
> Jesus, confirm my heart's desire
> To work, and speak, and think for Thee;
> Still let me guard the holy fire,
> And still stir up the gift in me.
>
> Ready for all thy perfect will,
> My acts of faith and love repeat;

Till death Thy endless mercies seal,
And make the sacrifice complete.[2]

Christ's sacrifice was meant for our salvation. Our sacrifice is meant for His service.

REFLECTION QUESTIONS

1. What is a sacrilege? What is its worst form, according to G. Campbell Morgan?
2. What is worship at its core? How does Luke 10:27 apply here?

PERSONAL APPLICATION

1. Pause to take stock. Ask yourself: Do I give God the best of my time? How will I give God the best of my energies today?
2. Use Wesley's words to guide you in prayer and refresh your spirit: "Jesus, confirm my heart's desire to work, and speak, and think for Thee; still let me guard the holy fire, and still stir up the gift in me."

ACKNOWLEDGMENTS

This book wasn't written in a few weeks. It was compiled from previously unpublished articles, essays, and newsletters I had written over many years. When the idea was presented to collect this material together into one book, there was only one person who could do that—my devoted research assistant of over twenty-five years, Danielle DuRant. She knows best what I have said and haven't said. It is a tribute to her diligence and commitment to me, to this ministry, and to my family. So, thank you, Danielle. You're the best.

Thank you also to my dear friend Joey Paul, whose ideas and guidance have shaped most of my writing. He's a master at his trade and has walked the distance with me. Thank you, Joey. You are loved.

To my publisher, my family, and my colleagues: without you all, none of this would be possible.

ACKNOWLEDGMENTS

Most of all, to my Lord and Savior, Jesus Christ, who inspires over a lifetime with truths that are inexhaustible.

RAVI ZACHARIAS
ATLANTA, GEORGIA, USA

ABOUT THE AUTHOR

When former skeptic and seventeen-year-old Ravi Zacharias heard the words of Jesus in John 14:19, "Because I live, you also will live," the trajectory of his life changed forever. In a time of helplessness and unbelief—when he was on a bed of suicide—the truth of Scripture brought hope to Zacharias, and he committed his life to Christ, promising, "I will leave no stone unturned in my pursuit of truth." Earlier in John 14, Jesus said, "I am the way and the truth and the life." This verse has become the cornerstone of Zacharias's ultimate mission as a Christian apologist and evangelist: to present and defend the truth of Jesus Christ that others may find life in Him. He is the founder and president of Ravi Zacharias International Ministries and has authored or edited more than twenty-five books in the fields of theology, apologetics, comparative religion, and philosophy, including *Can Man Live Without God?* and *Jesus Among Other*

Gods. He has mentored such individuals as bestselling author Nabeel Qureshi (*Seeking Allah, Finding Jesus*). Zacharias and his wife, Margie, have been married for more than forty-five years and have three grown children. They reside in Atlanta.

NOTES

CHAPTER 2: The Ultimate Calling

1. Quoted by Bobby Conway, *The Fifth Gospel* (Eugene, OR: Harvest House, 2014), 9.

CHAPTER 3: Point of Exclusion

1. Gilbert K. Chesterton, *What's Wrong with the World* (New York: Dodd, Mead and Company, 1912), 48.

CHAPTER 6: Christianity Without Christ?

1. John Stott, *Basic Christianity* (London: Intervarsity Press, 1971), 8.

CHAPTER 8: The Greatest Investment

1. A. W. Tozer, "Give Time to God," in *Mornings with Tozer: Daily Devotional Readings* (Chicago: Moody Publishers, 2015), reading for February 24.
2. Ibid.

CHAPTER 14: The Heart of God

1. Francis Thompson, *The Hound of Heaven* (Portland, ME: Thomas Mosher, 1902), 3.
2. Ibid., 16.

CHAPTER 15: What Happened to Your Hands?

1. Calvin Miller, *Spirit, Word, and Story* (Grand Rapids: Baker, 2005), 56–57.

CHAPTER 17: Justice and Virtue

1. "From George Washington to Edmund Randolph 28 September 1789," accessed 19 October 2018, https://founders.archives.gov/documents/Washington/05-04-02-0073.
2. Aristotle, *Nicomachean Ethics,* Book V, Chapter 1, accessed 23 July 2018, http://www.sacred-texts.com/cla/ari/nico/nico044.htm.
3. Henry Wadsworth Longfellow, *The Complete Poetical Works of Longfellow* (Boston: Houghton, Mifflin & Company, n.d.), 616.

CHAPTER 19: Who Owns Your Heart?

1. Daniel Goleman, *Emotional Intelligence* (New York: Bantam Books, 1994), 4.
2. David Gelernter, "How Hard Is Chess?" *TIME*, May 19, 1997.
3. Ibid.

CHAPTER 22: The Most Difficult Questions

1. Thomas Moore, *Dark Nights of the Soul* (New York: Penguin Random House, 2004), 3.

CHAPTER 26: All Things New

1. Sam Harris, "God's Dupes," *Los Angeles Times*, March 15, 2007.
2. Richard Dawkins, "Viruses of the Mind," *1992 Voltaire Lecture* (London: British Humanist Association, 1993), 9.

NOTES

CHAPTER 27: Does Prayer Matter
1. G. K. Chesterton, *Orthodoxy* (San Francisco: Ignatius Press, 1995), 87.

CHAPTER 28: The Spirit of Prayer
1. Quoted in Leonard Ravenhill, *Why Revival Tarries* (Minneapolis: Bethany Fellowship, 1959), 156.

CHAPTER 30: The Value of Something
1. G. K. Chesterton, *As I Was Saying*, Robert Knille, ed. (Grand Rapids: Eerdmans, 1985), 267.

CHAPTER 31: The Gift of Faith
1. G. K. Chesterton, Lecture 5: G.F. Watts, posted by Dale Ahlquist. Accessed 22 July 2018 at https://www.chesterton.org/lecture-5/.

CHAPTER 34: A Taste of Worship
1. William Temple, *Readings in St. John's Gospel* (London: Macmillan, 1940), 68.

CHAPTER 35: Living Temples
1. Daniel Bell, *The Cultural Contradictions of Capitalism* (New York: Basic Books, 1978), xv.

CHAPTER 38: Right Where We Are Wrong
1. Quoted in Dale Ahlquist, *G. K. Chesterton: The Apostle of Common Sense* (San Francisco: Ignatius Press, 2003).

CHAPTER 40: Regenerative Power
1. Carl H. Henry, *The Christian Mindset in a Secular Society* (Sisters, OR: Multnomah Press, 1984).
2. Ibid.

CHAPTER 41: Man of Sorrows

1. Oscar Wilde, *De Profundis* (New York: G. P. Putnam's Sons, 1911), 29.
2. Ibid.
3. Ibid.

CHAPTER 43: Scandal of the Cross

1. For an insightful article on this topic, see Abdu Murray, "Islam or Christianity: Reflections on God's Greatness," *Just Thinking Magazine* 24, no. 1, December 24, 2015, https://rzim.org/just-thinking/islam-or -christianity-reflections-on-gods-greatness/.
2. Attributed to E. H. Chapin and quoted under entry "Sin" in Tryon Edwards, ed., *A Dictionary of Thoughts: Being a Cyclopedia of Laconic Quotations from the Best Authors of the World, Both Ancient and Modern* (Detroit, MI: F. B. Dickerson Co., 1908), 527.

CHAPTER 44: Imagination and the Will

1. Graham Tomlin, "Profiles in Faith: Blaise Pascal (1623–1662)," accessed 5 November 2018, https://www.cslewisinstitute.org/webfm_send/609.

CHAPTER 45: Coping with Life's Turbulence

1. G. K. Chesterton, *The Thing* (New York: Dodd, Mead, 1944).

CHAPTER 46: Is It Worth It?

1. M. K. Gandhi, *Truth Is God* (Sabarmati, Ahmedabad: Navajivan Trust, 1994).

CHAPTER 47: Are You Lonely?

1. Thomas Wolfe, "God's Lonely Man" in *The Hills Beyond* (New York: Plume/New American Library, 1982), 146, 148.
2. Phillips Brooks, "O Little Town of Bethlehem," 1868.

CHAPTER 48: Finding the Perfect Gift

1. C. S. Lewis, *The Abolition of Man* (New York: HarperOne, 2001), 77.

CHAPTER 49: Safely into the Unknown

1. Quoted in Carl G. Vaught, *The Journey Toward God in Augustine's Confessions* (Albany, NY: State University of New York 2003), 23.
2. Minnie Lou Haskins, "God Knows," public domain.

CHAPTER 50: Peace Like a River

1. Horatio G. Spafford, "It Is Well with My Soul," 1873.
2. Ibid.
3. Peter Kreeft, *Catholic Christianity* (San Francisco: Ignatius Press, 2001), 185.

CHAPTER 52: Giving All

1. G. Campbell Morgan, *Malachi's Message for Today* (Eugene, OR: Wipf and Stock Publishers, 1998), 50.
2. Charles Wesley, "O Thou Who Camest from Above," 1762.